1954
MAKING A MARINE GRUNT WARRIOR

COLD WAR WARRIOR TRILOGY

1954
MAKING A MARINE PILOT WARRIOR

DAVID D. FERMAN

Copyright © David D. Ferman.

All rights reserved. No part of this book may be reproduced in any form or by any electronic or mechanical means, including information storage and retrieval systems, without permission in writing from the publisher, except by reviewers, who may quote brief passages in a review.

ISBN: 978-1-64669-972-8   (Paperback Edition)
ISBN: 978-1-64669-973-5   (Hardcover Edition)
ISBN: 978-1-64669-971-1   (E-book Edition)

Every person that I wrote about in my Cold War Warrior Trilogy was, or hopefully still is a living woman or man. However, in my trilogy (*1953—Making A Marine Grunt Warrior, 1954—Making A Marine Pilot Warrior, 1955—VAH-7, Secret Navy Atom Bomber Squadron*), I changed the names of several persons in each book to avoid embarrassing them or their relatives. I owe those wonderful old rascals that much for being such good friends back then, and such great material for these three books now. Given all possible choices today, I would not and could not write these true stories in any other way.

These books are interesting, somewhat humorous and didactic because they are absolutely true. All of the events, places, attitudes and opinions are factual. It has been 64 years since 1955, so some other old duffer's memories may differ from mine.

Book Ordering Information

Phone Number: 347-901-4929 or 347-901-4920
Email: info@globalsummithouse.com
Global Summit House
www.globalsummithouse.com

Printed in the United States of America

TABLE OF CONTENTS

I. INTRODUCTION

1. SEA STORIES 1
2. BACKSTORY 2

II. PENSACOLA FLIGHT TRAINING PROGRAM

1. "NEVER FLY HOME AGAIN" 12
2. THIRTY DAY TRAVEL ORDERS 13
3. HOW MANY STRIPES? 14
4. DARN JAPANESE COLOR TEST 15
5. "YA'LL ARE ALL OVERWEIGHT!" 16
6. "YOU GOTTA' BE KIDDING ME!" 16
7. RELEVANT MARINE QUOTE 19
8. MY BUDDY RUT 19
9. SSGT./NAVCAD WILLY BARNES 20
10. NAVCAD AL DRIMBA 22
11. DILBERT DUNKER 23
12. GORY GROUND-SCHOOL GRADUATION 24
13. MY FIRST SOLO FLIGHT 25
14. MEDIOCRE ANNAPOLIS ENSIGNS 26
15. LITTLE RED 28

16. LIFE GUARD CERTIFICATION 29
17. MARCELLUS MURDOCK—AVIATION PIONEER 30
18. ARAPAHO WAR CRY 32
19. DEBUTANT "GOOD GIRLS" 34
20. JUNKER SNJs 35
21. JUST ANOTHER DAY AT WORK 36
22. ENSIGN "KNOW-IT-ALL" BLEW HIS AVIATION CAREER 37
23. NAVCAD "GOT BUCK$" 38
24. "HOUKAH HEI:" A GOOD DAY TO DIE 40
25. NAVCAD LEON DYKUS 41
26. RUT'S HIGH SOCIETY WEDDING 42
27. LESSONS LEARNED IN BOXING CLASS 43
28. FOUL FRENCH CADETS 44
29. LEARN FROM ACCIDENT REPORTS 45
30. A FIRST-CLASS 1st CLASS SAILOR 46
31. FATAL TAKEOFF CRASH 47
32. PRINCIPLES-OF-FLIGHT CLASS 48
33. THE USUAL "UNUSUAL ATTITUDES" 48
34. AIR-TO-AIR COMBAT WAS FINALLY FUN. 50
35. CAPTAIN FISHER FROM THE BLACK SHEEP
    SQUADRON 52
36. "EVERY DOG HAS HIS DAY" 54
37. JIMMY BUFFETT'S DADDY'S MOONSHINE STILL 54
38. BOOMER THE SAILBOAT NUT 56
39. FIFTY THIRSTY NAVY "ADMIRALS" 57
40. THE ADMIRAL'S HAT FIT JUST FINE 58
41. NAVCAD PETE PETERSON OUT-MANEUVERED
    HIS SHRINK 59
42. CHECK FLIGHT SNAFU 61
43. NAVCAD "PUPPY DOG" MALOOF 63
44. NAVCAD "BARF BAG" MARKHAM 63
45. LOW AND SLOW 64
46. WHO SWIPED MY BASEBALL MITT? 66

47. FOREST FIRE BUGOUT 67
48. OLD SOCKS AND SEA BAGS.. 68
49. I GO MONO 72
50. STEALTH PRESCRIPTION GLASSES 76
51. BIG BAD BUBBA THE THUNDER BOOMER..................... 78
52. YA'LL HAIL THE SECRETARY OF THE NAVY................... 80
53. MERRY CHRISTMAS 1954 83
54. NIGHT FLYING NIGHTMARES 85
55. "WHAT A HELLOVA' WAY TO DIE." 86
56. GARBAGE MOUTHED WAVE.. 88
57. SKY KING.. 88
58. MARDI GRAS IN NEW ORLEANS 91
59. ADMIRAL CADET... 93
60. STRESS IS A BOOGER BEAR 96
61. I CRASHED, BURNED, AND DARN NEAR DROWNED..... 97
62. YOU SCRATCH MY BACK AND I'LL SCRATCH YOURS....... 106
63. AN OFFER I COULD NOT REFUSE 108
64. 1955: VAH-7 SECRET ATOM BOMBER SQUADRON........... 110
65. MILITARY AVIATION QUOTES....................................... 111

LIST OF FIGURES

Figure 1. Recruit Platoon 118, Day 3 in Boot Camp 3

Figure 2. Recruits Read Platoon 118 Graduation Certificates 4

Figure 3. The Author Played Semi-Pro Baseball to Win Contracts from the Boston Red Sox 4

Figure 4. Drill Instructors School, Class 19 Graduation 6

Figure 5. Firing Line, Camp Mathews, 500 Yard Line........................8

Figure 6. Marine Trained Rat..8

Figure 7. Recruit Platoon Final Inspection..9

Figure 8. Recruit Platoon Final Formation 9

Figure 9. SNJ, The Navy's Primary Training Aircraft in 1954......... 11

Figure 10. T-34, The USAF Primary Trainer Aircraft in 1954 (Navy version) 12

Figure 11. Confederate Air Corps Induction....................................31

Figure 12. Two-Plane Formation 37

Figure 13. George Bommerman (on the left), One of the Good Guys and Dave Ferman (on the right)...69

Figure 14. This Commendation Was Not Misplaced in the Shuffle......71

Figure 15. Plane Formation For Ultimate Confidence 79

Figure 16. Pre-flight Checkout with T-34 Aircraft............................84

Figure 17. Post-Flight Marketing Photograph 85

Figure 18. A Good Day To Thrash a Few Clouds.............................98

I. INTRODUCTION

1. SEA STORIES

If you did not read *1953: Making A Marine Grunt,* you should know that many civilians and boot camp recruits will ask: "What the heck is a sea story?"

An ancient and honorable tradition among the sea-going military services, sea stories are the most popular, highly preferred method of passing worthwhile information among the many millions of active duty, reserve and retired sailors and Marines. Make no mistake about it, authentic sea stories are always true (no scuttlebutt allowed), often humorous, usually first-person yarns about unusual and/or wondrous adventures such as grand and glorious victories, close calls, embarrassing faux pas, stupid mistakes, terrifying moments, dastardly deeds, galling disappointments, exotic locations, bawdy entertainment, hijinks when hammered, the women of (pick a place), "Dear John" letters and their often unforeseen consequences, commendations, awards, that 10 percent that never gets the word, regrettable foul ups, interesting trivia, or anything else worth mentioning that happened during active or reserve duty in the U.S. Marine Corps, the U.S. Navy, the U.S. Coast Guard or allied sister services, usually at sea or across the sea, but not always.

By the way, the sea story "voice" is always low-key conversational no matter what the subject except for matters of well-packaged gender. Sea stories come in a variety of sizes from a short vignette of only a few paragraphs to a dozen or more typed, single-spaced pages relative to a variety of categories such as those sea stories that typically:

a. Can usually be told comfortably in mixed adult company, including your mom, maiden aunt, and maybe even your Bible-thumping pastor, bless his or her heart.
b. Are told among consenting adults, but probably not your mom, maiden aunt or Bible-thumping pastor because very little if any adult content is usually deleted.
c. Are more appreciated by salty old "sea dog" veterans who were once, or will probably be in the same places or situations during his or her tours of duty.

But have no fear, the sea stories in this book are a blend of all but category "b" and are as true as memory permits. So sit back, relax, read on and enjoy. You will not need a Thesaurus.

Please note that this book is a mini-memoir and not a day-to-day diary. Although the sea stories herein are in chronological order, they are selected, generally short snippets that are often interspersed by days and even weeks on several occasions.

2. BACKSTORY

Aside from a few bumps along the way, Boot Camp at the U.S. Marine Corps Recruit Depot (MCRD), San Diego, California in the spring of 1953 was actually fairly enjoyable (figure 1). The Marines gave me the best rifle that I had ever fired, free ammunition, and let me shoot it for weeks at a time at the Camp Mathews rifle range. They also gave me three nutritious meals every day; some of which were fairly decent if you are not too picky and have a lot of condiments handy. But most important of all, they also gave me the opportunity to earn one of the most respected military uniforms on God's green earth. Who would not be proud to wear U.S. Marine "dress blues, spit-shined shoes and a light coat of oil?"

Figure 1. Recruit Platoon 118, Day 3 in Boot Camp

With all of the calisthenics, running and other physical and mental exercises all day every day with Recruit Platoon 118 (figure 2), otherwise known as the Wichita (Kansas) Platoon, I was probably in the best physical shape of my life. That included the prior football season when I was playing first string offensive/defensive end, kicking extra points and field goals, and punting for the Kansas junior college champion El Dorado Grizzlies; pulling old pipe in the Oil Patch during that sweltering Kansas summer and after-football weekends, as well as playing semi-professional baseball (figure 3). A second semester sophomore when I enlisted, I put a full football scholarship at Kansas State University for my junior and senior years on hold, as well as a professional baseball contract with the Boston Red Sox. Somehow I actually believed that I could easily get all of that good stuff back again after a three-year tour of duty in the Marines during the Korean War. Silly me.

Figure 2. Recruits Read Platoon 118 Graduation Certificates
(From left to right: Pfc's. William Ramirez, Gerald Casey, Erwin Littrell, Dave Ferman, and Floyd Snow)

Figure 3. The Author Played Semi-Pro Baseball to Win Contracts from the Boston Red Sox

Then some optimist in the chain of command must have believed that I could become a Grunt infantry officer, so they sent me to Drill Instructors' School as the first step in transitioning from enlisted to officer status. However, most of my platoon went to Korea to get even with the North Korean and Chinese communist hoards. Until that time, an applicant for DI School had to be at least a corporal (I was only a brand new Pfc.), have an officer's IQ (120 points or more), and preferably have combat experience. One out of three did not seem like a promising average to start down that road.

DI School was one of the most difficult and demanding schools in the Marine Corps. On average, about 50 percent of the highly qualified Marine warriors who were accepted by DI School either flunked out due to the constant written tests and pop quizzes every day, or the constant physical challenges, calisthenics and marching on the parade grounds. Except for the IQ requirement, I was definitely over my head and I knew it.

So I did not go on liberty breaks off the base, but memorized the large and very precise Landing Party Manual about all things Marine, and survived the many challenges to become one of only three graduates in my class (figure 4) who were immediately assigned to a recruit platoon although the ranking Gunnery Sergeant (five stripes: three up and two down) hated my guts because he thought I was having too much fun. Actually, when physically overexerted, I sounded like I was laughing every time I sucked-in air during extensive exercises when other guys were tossing their cookies and dropping out of the program. I figured what the heck, you can't please everybody all the time.

At that time, iconic Marine Colonel, later Major General, Lewis "Chesty" Puller declared that too many of his close air support pilots had not been as aggressive as he wanted during the "Frozen Chosin Reservoir" Campaign in the snow-covered mountains of far northern Korea. Chesty wanted some hard-charging enlisted Marine grunts to become pilots and show some of those ex-Ivy League fraternity boy pilots how close air support should be flown. As a result, 12 enlisted

Marines were initially chosen out of the 194,000 enlisted Marines in the Corps at that time. For some unfathomable reason, I was one of that dozen. Say what!

Figure 4. Drill Instructors School, Class 19 Graduation

In late September, I was transferred to Naval Air Station Moffett Field near San Jose, California to play football and basketball for the Red Raiders, work as a Military Policeman (MP) on patrol and at the Main Gate, and a Marine Guard at the super-secret Ames Laboratory where I was cleared to a Secret security clearance, but somehow I did not know about that clearance while waiting for my summons to Pensacola, Florida for pilot training. Don't ask me how; I don't have an answer for you.

The NAS Moffett Field Red Raiders played the Armed Forces Day Football Classic for 1953 on national TV. We lost because our best and only top notch running back broke his leg during war-game maneuvers a couple of days before the game. However, I lucked out because the TV announcer liked my punting a lot and said so repeatedly. Over the next few months, I received ten full football scholarships in the mail from Kansas, Nebraska, Missouri, Colorado, Oklahoma State (then A&M) and five other universities that were either on the wrong side of the Rocky Mountains or the Mississippi River. Of course, I chose the wrong school for the wrong reason, but that's another story for another time.

The best part about Moffett Field was finally receiving my Advanced Combat Training with elements of the famous 5th Marine Brigade of the 1st Marine Division that mauled the three Chinese Divisions that were assigned to destroy the 1st Marine Division during the "Frozen Chosin Reservoir" Campaign in North Korea during the terribly harsh winter of 1950/51. Ooooo-raaah! I loved every minute of my combat training in the mountains of northern California. I could not have had better teachers or better examples than the veterans of the 5th Marine Brigade.

As the junior DI with Platoon 205, I worked long hours (18 hours/7 days a week: there was no such thing as overtime when the junior DI) to teach our 75 recruits how to: obey orders; do the "five S's" between reveille and the morning calisthenics before breakfast; march and run together long distances in precise formations; master the basics of being a Marine; iron military creases into their Class "A" shirts (i.e., blouses) and trousers; hike 20 miles into the southern California mountains with full battle gear and only one canteen of water each; shoot M1 rifles accurately at 200, 300, and 500 yard ranges (figure 5); throw hand grenades and skewer bad guys on the pointy ends of our bayonets if they are dumb enough to get that close (figure 6); become squared-away Marine recruits who have mastered everything required of them (figure 7); then graduate from Boot Camp (figure 8) as basic trained United States Marines.

Figure 5. Firing Line, Camp Mathews, 500 Yard Line

Figure 6. Marine Trained Rat

Figure 7. Recruit Platoon Final Inspection

Figure 8. Recruit Platoon Final Formation

II. PENSACOLA FLIGHT TRAINING PROGRAM

I could not have picked a worse time to enter the U.S. Navy's Pilot Training Program at Pensacola, Florida in March of 1954. Those pre-World War II SNJ Texan basic pilot-training aircraft (figure 9) were worn out from the rigors of constant simulated and actual aircraft-carrier operations for far too long. Various parts such as engine nacelles were falling off SNJ fusillades in flight, flight-control cables would pop off the roller tracks, metal fatigue took its toll, and accidents were all too common. At least a dozen pilots—students and instructors—were killed during my first year of pilot training.

At that time, the student pilots in the U.S. Air Force Pilot Training Program were flying the new, much improved Beechcraft T-34 Mentor (figure10) and suffered no fatalities. Until Beechcraft satisfied their USAF production contract and switched over to produce the Navy version of the T-34 in 1956, the Navy struggled to train us in those sad, old, worn-out SNJs.

Figure 9. SNJ, The Navy's Primary Training Aircraft in 1954

Figure 10. T-34, The USAF Primary Trainer Aircraft in 1954 (Navy version)

1. "NEVER FLY HOME AGAIN"

"Never Fly Home Again" was a popular although eerie, but certainly appropriate Navy Cadet (NavCad) drinking song that was sung to the tune of "The Battle Hymn of the Republic. We who flew those old "gut shot" SNJ aircraft were fully aware of just how dangerous those old crates could be. When one of our guys crashed and "bought the farm" (i.e., the victim's beneficiary received $10,000), many of us gathered in the NavCad beer bar after supper, toasted the unfortunate pilot(s) into the night, then tried to not mention him or them again.

"Never Fly Home Again"

"Here's a toast to those who wear the Navy Wings of Gold.
They are fearless flying heroes who are trained both well and bold.
They carouse a bit and party, and drink quantities untold.
And they'll all fly home again.

"Glory, glory hallelujah.
Glory, glory hallelujah.
Glory, glory hallelujah.
And they'll all fly home again.

"He was coming from the "90" when he got a little slow,
He ignored the pleading paddles of the frantic L.S.O.
When he finally added throttle, he was just a little low,
And he'll never fly home again.

Refrain:

"Gory, gory, what a hell of a way to die.
Gory, gory, what a hell of a way to die.
Gory, gory, what a hell of a way to die,
And he'll never fly home again.

"Little bits of wreckage scattered o'er the Navy base,
And a little pool of blood to mark his final resting place.
Now he wears a Mark-8 gunsight where he used to wear a face,
And he'll never fly home again.
(Repeat refrain)

"There was blood upon the runway, there was blood upon his boots.
There was blood upon the remnants of his summer flying suit.
They scraped him from the cockpit, and they wrapped him in his 'chute,
And he'll never fly home again.
(Repeat refrain)
(Then slowly)

"Ten – thousand – dollars – going – home – to – his – wife.
Ten – thousand – dollars – in – exchange – for – his – life.
More – damned – money - and – less – family – strife.
And he'll never fly home again.

2. THIRTY DAY TRAVEL ORDERS

A commercial flight from San Francisco, California to Pensacola, Florida, by United or Continental Airlines should take no longer than eight hours as the crow flies. Even with a couple of stopovers along the way, that trip by commercial airliner should take no longer than a day. However, for some undeclared reason, the U.S. Marine Corps allowed me 30 days of leave and a whole potful of money to make that journey.

So I stopped in Denver for three days to meet my little cousin Amy's "really beautiful" roommate. She certainly was, but that was a romantic nonstarter. So I moved along to my hometown, Wichita, Kansas, to spend some time with family, a few close friends, and several zaftig home-town beer-serving wenches.

After a couple of weeks in my old stomping grounds on R&R, Cpl. George Bailey picked me up in his Oldsmobile coup, and then we drove to Tulsa, Oklahoma, to pick-up Pfc. Tucker whose dad was the Mayor of Tulsa. With recess getting short, we passed up a huge party at the Mayoral mansion, drove down to Irving, Texas, just outside of Dallas where we picked up Cpl. Joe Bolling, and headed for New Orleans where we took in every bar and show in the French Quarter for a couple of days before heading northeast to Pensacola, Florida. Since we arrived in town fairly late in the day, we stayed at the Carousel Bar until it closed, and then the four of us slept in George's Oldsmobile for the rest of the night and reported for duty at NAS Pensacola at 08:00 the next morning.

3. HOW MANY STRIPES?

That's when I got my first of several surprises that day. When I was promoted to corporal back at NAS Moffett Field, I had my new stripes sewn only on my winter uniforms—because it was winter in northern California—to save some money to spend on girls, girls, girls and 10-cent beers in Denver and Wichita. I had figured that I did not need to spend that money to put my stripes on my summer uniforms until March. Heck, maybe Mom could do the job free gratis on her 1920's sewing machine.

Well, Mom's old free sewing machine was out of service, and when I got to Pensacola, darned if the summer Uniforms of the Day weren't already in order in downtown Florida. So I had to dig my summer uniforms out of the depths of my sea bag and wear them even though they still had Pfc. stripes on them. Damn! I figured that was no big deal since I could borrow a few dollars from George and Joe D. and have my corporal's stripes sewn on at the Post Exchange, then pay my pals back on the next payday. What the heck, I was still a Marine corporal with or without whatever was temporarily on my sleeves.

4. DARN JAPANESE COLOR TEST

Although hung over and pretty much dragging our fannys, naturally, the second surprise of the day was to retake our eyeball tests all over again. Long story short, I flat flunked that Japanese color test where a Marine Corporal who is color blind will see one set of numbers composed of many colored dots, and Marine Corporals with normal eyes will see another set of numbers in that same stew of dots. Naturally I picked the wrong numbers, and flunked the eye test flat. Aw well, there goes flight training. It was fun while it lasted.

The Corpsman in charge of testing, a grizzled old Chief Petty Officer, was sitting at the central paper shuffling desk while eating a box of store-bought fried chicken (the first such meal that I had ever seen) and looking through the two-inch-thick folder of my accumulated medical records since the day I joined the Marines back in Kansas City. He could see that I had passed the color tests in Wichita, at Kansas City, at MCRD San Diego, at the Navy hospital at San Diego, and at El Toro.

That crusty old Chief was perplexed to say the least. Finally, he stared intently at me as I stood in front of him, put down his fried chicken leg and said: "These are your medical records, aren't they?" Before I could answer him, Cpl. George Bailey popped up behind me and said: "What do you expect, Chief? Dave has been partying for a whole month, and he stayed up all last night."

The Chief looked at me like as if his head was about to explode, studied my latest color test one more time and the others in my medical records, said "f*** it," stamped the eye test check-off list as "PASSED," and I became a Marine NavCad. It was indeed a full life. Fortunately, salty old Navy Chiefs usually prefer to avoid explaining any data diffugalties to their bosses.

5. "YA'LL ARE ALL OVERWEIGHT!"

Then that afternoon during our next surprise, flight physicals, a very prim, prissy, pucker faced middle-aged civilian lady informed us that every one of us was overweight except for one skinny little civilian guy who had some kind of a malformed structure in his rib cage that was actually concave in the center of his solar plexus. I had not seen that physical anomaly before or since, and he looked just flat emaciated overall as well. She told the rest of us in no uncertain terms that the skinny guy was the only one of us whose weight was right according to her height charts.

I double-dog doubted that because I had recently gone through physically challenging boot camp, Drill Instructors School's even more physical and mental challenges, played college level football and basketball, and was probably in the best shape of my life at about 215 pounds.

The other Marine NavCads were in comparable conditions, and probably in the best shape of their lives as well. So we all just flat ignored that old gal and never mentioned her quirky theories again, much like the way I dealt with my prior head injuries: I dealt with them, recovered, moved on and did not look back.

By the way, the emaciated guy with the concave rib cage dropped out within a couple of weeks. He had very little energy and could not keep up the pace with us overweight "fat" guys.

6. "YOU GOTTA' BE KIDDING ME!"

The next surprise was the biggest and baddest surprise imaginable; a previously unmentioned show-stopper that ruined my day. The Navy demanded that we enlisted Marine grunts assigned to this new program had to be discharged from my Marine Corps and re-enlisted in the U.S. Navy Reserves as an essential part of Naval Aviation Flight Training. That was their hard and fast rule, and there was no wiggle room around it although Marine officers were immune from that stupid hog wash.

Say what! That crap just did not make it with a bunch of gung ho former Marine Drill Instructors and combat veterans. Before any of us

1954 MAKING A MARINE PILOT WARRIOR

Marines knew what was happening, a swarm of Personnel-pogue Navy officers and their office pinkies herded us into a closed conference room and began processing our discharges as if we had no say in the matter.

When I finally understood that this unthinkable situation was happening to me, I dug-in my heels and called a halt to my part of that unacceptable rain dance. As I made very clear, I was a by-God U.S. Marine, a decorated 0911 Drill Instructor, and not a doggoned anchor-clanking sailor. Period…end of the conversation. By that time, my pals, Corporals George Bailey and Joe Bolling, who had already signed on with NavCad Program, were encouraging (more like pleading with) me to stay with them at Pensacola. However, all I wanted was a ticket on the next bus out of town.

Someone must have had his honor or his manhood bet on us, because the Navy Officers kept me corralled and the single door to the conference room locked until a tall, Hollywood handsome Marine Lieutenant Colonel sporting aviator wings and five rows of ribbons showed up and stroked the main source of trouble, me, a lot more than I probably rated. This Marine "officer and gentleman" assured me that this temporary duty assignment was nothing but a Navy formality to get young enlisted Marines into Naval flight training. He also assured me that after I earned my "Navy Wings of Gold," I would be automatically transferred back into the Marine Corps, and if anything bad nasty like crashing or flunking out should happen along the way, the Marines would take me back eee-mediately if not sooner.

He also assured me that my prior time in the Marines, plus the USNR aviation training time would be counted against my final Marine enlistment time if I wanted to be discharged after 36 months.

In fact, that light colonel allowed that except for specific dress uniforms-of-the-day during formal formations, I was cleared to wear my "Marine green" uniforms with Marine ribbons (Drill Instructor, National Defense as well as Letter of Commendation when it finally caught up with me) and shooting medal with Naval Aviation Cadet (NavCad) collar insignia and rank at the various fields within the training command, on leave, and on liberty. As he said: "the Marine umbilical was not cut, it was just temporarily obscured."

So what the heck. This impressive aviator had given his word, and I was not accustomed to questioning senior Marine officers. So grudgingly, I finally capitulated and fell into line with the rest of the Marine NavCads. After all of that assurance, what could possibly go wrong?

Basically everything. In hind sight, I should have paid more attention to my Marine DD-214 as separation papers. However, by the time that I finally acquiesced and go ahead with my fellow Marines, every other Navy Personnel pogue in the room had wrapped up his or her assigned Marine applicants and was leaving or had left for the day.

In the rush to catch up, I should have asked why that "sweet-talking Yankee carpetbagger" Personnel officer and gentleman was asking me questions like when and where I had enlisted, the military school that I attended, my home address in Wichita, Kansas, and all of the other information that was already available on my DD-214. Couldn't he read what was already written on my original DD-214? In the rush to complete everything, I never did get a decent answer.

After waiting several months, I figured that my promised Letter Of Commendation should have been processed. My Commanding Officer back at NAS Moffett Field wasn't the kind of guy to promise that award and then cancel that award. Both he and I and several hundred others back at Moffett knew that if I hadn't jerked those two darn-near naked sailors out of that shower room and forced them down the stairs against their wills and out of that blazing building, they would have been cut off from escape paths and burned to death. The shower room where I found those guys was totally destroyed in that raging fire.

In all of the rushing around to get everything done before supper, I forgot to mention that I really was a bona fide U.S. Marine corporal, but that was also on my original DD-214 so I didn't give it no nevermind. Then the Personnel officer and his assistant stuffed all of my papers into a briefcase willy nilly, said "sign here" and they were out of there like bats out of Hades. I guess the "O" Club had just opened for Happy Hour. However, I did not get to see those papers again for about 14 years, long after the Military Records Building fire in St. Louis, Missouri had supposedly destroyed them. By then. I did not give a flip, and apparently, neither did the Navy Department.

7. RELEVANT MARINE QUOTE

"A Marine is a Marine. I set that policy two weeks ago. There's no such thing as a former Marine. You're a Marine, just in a different uniform, and you're in a different phase of your life. But you'll always be a Marine because you went to Parris Island, San Diego or the hills of Quantico. There's no such thing as a former Marine."

General James F. Amos, the 35th Commandant of the U.S. Marine Corps.

8. MY BUDDY RUT

Later that same evening, my good buddy, Marine Cpl/NavCad Richard U. Temple (RUT) and I went out to the pier on the bay to cool down, unwind and try to get oriented within that huge Navy base. As we stood at the deep-water end of the long Navy pier, a two-year old baby boy toddled over the side of the pier and fell about 10 feet into Pensacola Bay. With no time to get rid of our shoes, billfolds, etc., RUT and I jumped into the bay right behind the baby. I grabbed the little fellow before he resurfaced in about 12 feet of water and handed him to RUT, who then handed him up a long ladder to his dad, an older guy who was wearing Marine dungarees with no rank showing.

Since our Class "A" Marine summer khaki uniforms, spit-shined shoes, wallets, etc. were already soaked, RUT and I enjoyed the opportunity to goof around in the water, fully clothed, and cooled off for about five minutes or so before climbing out of the water. The dad, mom and his whole family thanked us enthusiastically, hugged us and shook our hands all around a couple of times. Heck, at least we made some new friends on our first day there.

So what was the surprise? Well, about a week later, RUT and I were part of three NavCad classes swimming simultaneously in the base indoor pool for orientation. Normally only one class would be in the pool at a time. But this time, the whole Olympic pool was over-crowded with showoffs swimming over, under, and around each other, so RUT and I said to heck with that, avoided the mad melee by grabbing a couple of non-swimmer flotation cans, and floated peacefully on our backs in the middle of the hectic splashathon with the other non-swimmers.

That is, we did until the Head Dog swimming instructor ordered us to take off our flotation devices and swim like everybody else, because he knew that we could swim. Of course, we both denied that, but when we looked closer at him, we both recognized him. Our boss swimming instructor was the father of the baby who fell into the bay a week before. Maybe if we had given that baby a few more seconds free in the water, he might have swam off doing the Australian crawl or back stroke and left us far behind in his wake.

Nevertheless, we were busted so we accepted our lumps like good Marines and gave up our flotation cans.

9. SSGT./NAVCAD WILLY BARNES

I really lucked out in Pre-Flight Ground School at NAS Pensacola. One of my new friends and roommate was Marine Staff Sergeant Willy Barnes. This decorated war hero had been an enlisted plane captain/mechanic /crewman on one particular USMC DC-3 cargo airplane during the series of vicious battles around the frozen Chosin Reservoir.

If you do not know about the epic battles as the Marines fought their way through the North Korean mountains in the dead of winter while outnumbered three or four to one, you really should read about one of the greatest battles in the history of warfare. My tour of duty at NAS Moffett Field with remnants of the 5th Marine Brigade was like also living and training with elements of the Marines who fought and won at Guadalcanal or Iwo Jima. Those guys were Marine icons as a unit, but generally unheralded as individuals. That's a darned shame, but that was the general temperament in the USA at that time.

Anyway, during that incredible series of battles, Staff Sgt. Barnes' DC-3 flew back and forth to the battle grounds numerous times each day through freezing blizzards and whiteouts in support of the grunt Marines fighting the hordes of Chinese on the ground. That heroic flight crew flew constant supply and relief missions for several weeks, often eating and sleeping aboard the aircraft so the Marines on the ground would not run out of crucial supplies.

The exhausted pilots would often take-off from a Marine airbase in South Korea, then collapse into their makeshift bunks for some essential shuteye while SSgt. Barnes flew the DC-3 straight and level to the moving battle area in northern North Korea. Then the pilots either dropped their cargo in parachutes packs or else landed on barely adequate, make-shift runways. The mud Marines quickly unloaded the new supplies, put their wounded aboard the airplane, and the pilots took off again while all of the bad-nasty ChiComs in the area used them for target practice.

As soon as the DC-3 was at cruising altitude again, SSgt. Barnes would often take over and fly the plane straight and level back to the USMC air base in South Korea while the pilots caught up on their meals and sleep again. These tenacious heroes ate sack lunches and took turns flying the DC-3 in subfreezing, stormy conditions until the Marines on the ground were finally safe at the port city of Hungnam under the umbrella of Navy shipboard heavy artillery (from 5-inch up to 14- and 16-inch diameter shells) from a U.S. Navy battleship, cruisers and even the tin-can destroyers who sailed close to the beaches to make up for their comparative lack of range from their smaller ordnance with their more rapid-firing naval artillery. Within that withering fire storm, no ChiCom grunt would dare to tread.

Although tottering on the upper age limit for NavCad training (27 years old), SSgt. Barnes really wanted to be a Naval Aviator. He had proven that he could fly a multi-engine airplane under extreme stress, so the Navy and the Marine Corps made an exception for him. He had more than earned the right to give it a try.

That was pure good luck for me because SSgt. Barnes knew Navy/Marine radial engines backward and forward, and he didn't mind taking the time to get me checked out enough to pass the final test where some malfunction was introduced into a running radial engine in the test lab, and each NavCad had to diagnose the various problems and then correct them. I'm not sure that I would have passed those engine tests if not for SSgt. Barnes.

Unfortunately he was not very good at celestial navigation, principles of flight, and other math-heavy classroom courses like that so, although I helped him as much as I could, SSgt. Barnes did not make the cut out of pre-flight ground school. I guess that he was a far better teacher than I was. It was an honor to know him. Gung ho, SSgt. Willie Barnes, and Semper Fi for good measure. He was a fine example of a very good Marine.

10. NAVCAD AL DRIMBA

Before I became the NavCad "Fearless Leader," I had another terrific roommate and good friend who helped me pass my swimming tests. I could swim, and I had actually pulled several friends out of the sand-dredged local swimming ponds back in Wichita, Kansas. However, I was far from being the certified lifeguard that the Navy required each NavCad to be.

Cadet Al Drimba was a squared-away former Navy enlisted man who had completed his four-year Navy enlistment at about the same time as we graduated from ground school at NAS Pensacola Mainside. By the rules at that time—I understand that they are probably different now—Al could therefore resign and go home at any time that he wished. However, Al was a very promising pilot who took to flying like a fish takes to water. I thought that Al was born to fly. Like SSgt. Willy Barnes, he was unshakable.

Speaking of water, Al was the best swimmer in almost any swimming pool, anytime, anywhere. Some of us thought that he should try out for the Olympics. He and his family were also accomplished skin divers and deep sea divers as well. When I was having a hard time passing the final test—a half-pool Australian crawl followed by an abrupt surface dive and then swim the other half of the Olympic-sized swimming pool under water—Al and I worked together for several days to get me qualified. He was the instructor; I was the instructed. The underwater part was kicking my donkey until Al gave me a pair of swimming goggles, and then he swam along beside me until I finally touched the far wall. He knew that I would not quit before he quit, and he was right.

Al had a lot of stories about himself and his dad searching for sunken Spanish galleons in and around the Florida Keys; particularly one wreck that was supposedly ballasted with gold bars. Over pitchers of cold beer and more rum-and-Coca Colas than I care to recall, Al told great stories and I kinda', sorta', maybe believed most of what he said. That's a pretty good average for a new friend who told such wild, exciting sea stories.

The thing was that on many weekends, Al would travel all of the way from Pensacola to the Keys (that's a heck of a long way and I had no clue how he did it or how he got the clearances) to sector search an ever-decreasing area for that prize galleon. He told me that if he and his family ever found it, he would call in, resign from the NavCads, and apply for his honorable discharge.

About six months after starting the NavCad Flight Program, one Monday morning, Al called the Training Command from Key West and resigned. I never saw him again. However, several months after that I was reading an experimental weekly news magazine much like *"Look Magazine,"* but it was considerably smaller so that it could be carried in a shirt pocket to read in the john. The lead story was about one of the most successful Spanish galleon hunters in the Caribbean Sea. His name: Al Drimba.

Where I come from, we do something and then we talk about it. Al had made it work the other way around. Good for him.

11. DILBERT DUNKER

I loved the Dilbert Dunker—a mockup SNJ cockpit with a blunt forward bulkhead—and I rode it like a carnival attraction every chance I could get it. Dressed in flight gear with oversized rubber shoes (one size fits all), flight helmet, mockup parachute, Mae West flotation vest and all the rest of that gear for flight over water, each cadet would ride the dunker down a long set of rails, hit the water fairly hard at a fairly high speed that sprayed water all of the way to the other end of the Olympic pool, and then continue on the rails to a depth of about 15 feet as the dunker inverted completely. Once ol' Dilbert came to a stop, the cadet would release and get out of his safety harness, kick off downward to clear the inverted cockpit, and then swim to the surface.

More than a few just-out-of-college civilian cadets and brand new shave-tail ensigns panicked, popped their Mae West backup flotation vests while still inverted in the cockpit, which caused them to float up into the floor boards of the inverted aircraft mockup, and then those dummies would go berserk and had to be cut out of their gear and pulled to the surface by two standby Navy divers who watched each operation from under water. Not one Marine ever suffered that debilitating indignity. I would have chewed a hole in the Mae West flotation vest before I would ever signal a standby Navy diver to deactivate my Mae West to save my Marine backside. "Semper Fi" is not just a hollow motto, it is a way of life.

We also had a test whereby we would wear the same gear except for the Mae West flotation device, jump off the high diving board, remove our shoes, shuck our trousers to make a jury-rigged flotation device by tying a knot in each leg at the cuff end, flip the trousers overhead to capture enough air to make a serviceable flotation device, and then float for about five minutes to show any skeptics that the readymade flotation device actually worked.

Later, when I was overseas in the Mediterranean Sea, a Marine mechanic fell overboard from a blacked-out pitching flight deck late at night. No one knew that he was gone until about half a day later. Then they found him still floating with his trouser flotation device about a day later. He was still giving it his best shot. He must have done that air refill trick hundreds of times since he probably had flipped his trousers over his head to refill them with air about every five to ten minutes. Later, I heard that he had lost his preference for saltwater toffee. Who'da thunk it?

12. GORY GROUND-SCHOOL GRADUATION

After the first eight hectic weeks of orientation and ground school, our NavCad class was graduating to begin flight operations with a formal battalion formation of all ground school classes on the huge, grassy parade grounds. The second in command to George Baily at that time, I made sure that the entire ceremony was conducted perfectly on the parade ground, and that the commands were loud, in cadence, and crisp. It did not hurt that we had nine Marines in that class, and most if not all were class officers. All nine had graduated from DI School, and two of us had been working drill instructors with Marine recruit platoons back at MCRD San Diego.

With flags flying, sabers flashing and perfect precision, we were putting on quite a demonstration of parade ground proficiency when we all heard a loud BANG overhead as two of our SNJ training aircraft collided, were locked together by the impact, and were falling into the bay. As we watched the two planes falling as one, only one parachute could be seen. Welcome to the Pensacola Flight Training Command. Be careful, y'all because this is not the U.S. Air Force.

13. MY FIRST SOLO FLIGHT

After about 18 to 20 hours of flight time in the SNJ Texan primary trainer aircraft (figure 9) with Lt. Paul Stretch, my instructor pilot in the back seat, I was ready for my first solo flight. After a potful of high and low altitude practice, I landed at a huge grassy auxiliary field near the Florida/Alabama border, and Lt. Stretch crawled out and headed for the temporary shade of a group of folding chairs arrayed with cold drinks and tables under a couple of beach umbrellas. This was the real thing, so I went over my takeoff checklist, set my propeller rpm and rapidly added power as the aircraft—now my aircraft—rolled forward and then left the surly bonds of this earth behind as I headed for 500 feet of altitude in the racetrack landing pattern. Hardly airborne a couple of minutes, I was about to make my first solo landing. Confident but a little nervous, I wanted this first solo landing in my pilot's logbook to be a good one.

However, as I joined the standard race track landing pattern with a few other cadets and began to descend in a left-hand turn at the 90-degree point from the touchdown marker, a NavCad friend in the SNJ just in front of me, who was also on his first solo flight, did not line up with the duty runway soon enough on the less-than-clearly marked north-south landing markers painted on that grass field. Apparently striving for perfection, he made his final course correction way too late and much too low to land on the center stripe at the last seconds in his final approach. Then, instead of flying with his wings straight and level as he touched down in a full-stall landing, his left wing was lower than it should have been at the last moment; he was probably still adjusting his approach because the markers were a bit hard to see in the grass.

As I watched from right behind him at about the middle of the last 90-degree left turn, he dragged his wingtip as he tried too late to ease further to the left, cart-wheeled the airplane on the grassy runway, the SNJ flipped over, hit the ground inverted, and blew up as I added full power and aborted my landing. Welcome to the intrinsic danger of aircraft carrier type landings, especially for student pilots landing on poorly marked grass fields.

With my throat in a knot and my stomach churning, I ascended to 1,000 feet and orbited the grass field while the crash crew and the Navy corpsmen did their grizzly jobs. Finally, the ground crew setup another parallel grass runway for landing about 60 yards or so to the right of the initial runway. As I dropped into the 500-foot altitude landing pattern again, I heard my orders to land and then stop to pick-up my instructor pilot who was waiting for me. It was time to go for broke.

With the smoke still rising from the wreckage and the ambulance still parked as close to the blackened grass as possible, I made my first landing on my first pass as my instructor pilot stood by the newly marked grass runway and graded my approach and landing on his note pad.

My first solo landing as a NavCad pilot was Pucker City; but conversely being torn between the sadness of losing a new friend, and the thrill of finally getting that first solo landing out of the way, that one of many landings sticks with me today.

"Gory, gory, what a hell of a way to die," was ringing in my mind.

14. MEDIOCRE ANNAPOLIS ENSIGNS

None of us Marine NavCads were impressed with the recent graduates of the U.S. Naval Academy at Annapolis, Maryland. We thought that we would be, but after a series of very disappointing experiences, we were not. When we formed our first flight-training squadron at Whiting Field, it was comprised of seven Marine cadets, three French cadets who had graduated from the French Naval Academy, and six newly graduated ensigns from our Naval Academy at Annapolis. Naturally, we former grunts were a bit apprehensive because all classes were graded on a curve, and the bottom of the curve was a bad place to be if you dream of making Naval Aviation your career.

However, when the final grades were posted eight weeks later, the seven Marines were at the top of the class, the three French cadets were next, and the six Naval Academy ensigns were at the tail end of the academic curve. Amazing? You danged betcha' that was amazing. We never would have guessed that despite being graded on a curve, none of the ensigns at the bottom of our class were disqualified. That was not the way it worked out for SSgt. Willie Barnes back in Ground School.

Not only that, but the flying segment of the syllabus was even worse. Those ensigns were, as a group, mediocre to lousy pilots, most of whom should have been dropped from the program; but for some cockamamie reason, they were not. That was our introduction to the wonderful world of preferential ring knocking (i.e., when an Annapolis school ring is knocked on a table top so the other guys will be reminded that the knocker graduated from Annapolis).

There was one particularly inept ensign student pilot who was the bane of my formation flying existence because he always seemed to wind up on my wing in aerial formations, and he could not hold his position worth a damn even when flying straight and level. Flying with a ten-foot step down between our aircraft, in a turn he was invariably all over the sky except where he should be. That gets darned hairy very darned quickly. I could not understand how he was able to stick around, but he did.

One day, we were flying a six-plane formation, I was number 5 and he was number 6. Every time we went into a turn, he was all over my air space until finally my wingtip kissed his canopy over the rear cockpit of his aircraft, which slightly jammed my wingtip against my aileron. That made just flying the SNJ a bit more difficult, and flying in formation impossible. So I broke out of the formation because my airplane was no longer as nimble as the rest in the formation, and that could be dangerous. I kid you not.

Despite a bit of difficulty, I was able to get back to the base by using throttle adjustments and rudder pedal a bit more than usual to get lined up with the runway about 10 miles out, and then let down in a straight line without too much aileron action until the wheels kissed the tarmac at the second third of the runway. About 20 seconds later, I found myself parked in the rough just a bit beyond the end of the duty runway. When talking about foretelling bad things to come downstream, that was a pretty darned good example. However, it did boost my confidence in the airplane as well as myself as a developing pilot.

15. LITTLE RED

Little Red—not the red-headed guy from Marine DI School—was the smallest, skinniest guy I have ever seen in the Armed Forces. He had no fat whatsoever, and he did not float worth a hoot. That was unfortunate because he could not swim worth a hoot either. That got fairly hairy for him when we practiced jumping off the high diving board into the training pool in shoes, shirt and trousers, and then swimming the length of the Olympic pool to satisfy another NavCad requirement.

After swallowing a lot of water several times because the 12-foot long rescue pole was never put within his reach while there was even an outside chance that he might recover on his own. No dummy, Little Red finally figured out the drill with the pole. Unable to swim worth a flip, unable to get himself back to the surface, nevertheless, that brave little guy would climb the ladder up the tower, walk to the end of the diving board and, without hesitation, he would jump off perfectly with one hand over his nose and the other protecting his crotch from the impact of hitting the water.

Every single time, he would hit the water cleanly with his feet first, sink to the bottom of the pool, immediately stop struggling and hang limp in the water so that the instructors would quickly put the rescue pole in front of him. He would then scramble up the pole like a monkey in the jungle. That whole rain dance was hard to watch over and over again, so we were all relieved when little Red finally washed out of the program and probably did not have to swim again with a gaggle of loudmouthed yahoos yelling crazy loud to encourage him. Little Red was a very brave guy but a lousy swimmer.

16. LIFE GUARD CERTIFICATION

Lifesaving was a big part of the swimming qualifications, so after completion of the course, we were all qualified to be Life Guards on the beach or at the several swimming pools on the base. What a slick racket that was. If you can't make time with the beach bunnies when playing with those cards, you might as well fold 'em and move on down the road.

I had been training to jump into the deep end of the Olympic pool, control a struggling victim from behind, and then tow the victim the length of our indoor Olympic pool. I was just barely passing when I took my final test. However, the "victim" that I had been practicing with was almost as skinny as Little Red but about six feet tall, and I was exhausted each time I tried to tow him the length of the pool. That was a bummer, and it really had me worried.

However, when I arrived for the final rescue test, my usual test "victim" was absent, so I was assigned a fairly pudgy guy who was about as tall as myself but still had some of his baby fat. Good grief, I just knew that I was in deep kim shee. However, as a Marine I was honor bound to accept what I was given, and give it my best shot even if I drowned both of us in the process.

So off we went, headed for the far wall. And true to my worst fears, he was initially even harder to control and then tow than my usual "victim." In fact, I had not gone very far when I had to stop to catch my breath. But unlike my previous experiences under those circumstances, I found myself actually leaning on my victim who was floating on his back somewhat like a log. The rest of the test was a laugher because I was leaning on him to rest every 20 feet or so. The lesson learned, if you and I ever have to save a couple of people struggling in the water, I will take the chubby one every time.

My Mama did not raise any fools.

17. MARCELLUS MURDOCK—AVIATION PIONEER

Marcellus Murdock was the owner and publisher of one of my home-town newspapers—The Wichita Eagle—and an old-time aviation pioneer from the 1920s and 1930s. When he visited the Pensacola Training Command, it seemed that every flag officer in the area, including the Admiral in charge of the Training Command, were lined up to have a Kodak Moment taken with Marcellus Murdock, and then buy another round of popskull in his honor at the Officers' Club. But then, everybody that was anybody had to get back to other events, so the Admiral tapped the NavCad Battalion Commander, yours truly, and ordered me to escort that old guy on a three-day Cook's Tour, and to spare no expense or "Wow event." Okay, I could do that. At Pensacola, we were up to our giblets in "Wow events."

So for three long days and nights, I took Marcellus Murdock and his reporter/photographer peon around the entire command: NAS Pensacola Mainside, NAS Whiting, NAS Sauffley, NAS Cecil Field and even on the USS Monterey, a small WWII jeep aircraft carrier where about a dozen NavCads were getting their first taste of making "touch and go" landings while the ship was underway in the Caribbean. Everywhere we went, Murdock had a good, long look at everything of interest, he was wined and dined like visiting royalty, and he gladly posed for "grip and grin" photographs with everybody and anybody we could corral.

I must have made a fairly decent impression on ol' Marcellus because the Wichita Eagle newspaper ran a full page story with beaucoup photographs that described in great detail my experiences as a Marine DI and as a Marine NavCad. Not only that, but a couple of weeks after Marcellus returned to Wichita, I received a formal induction into the famed Confederate Air Corps (figure 11), which had originated with Pappy Boyington's Black Sheep Squadron within the Cactus Air Corps ("Cactus" was the code name for Guadalcanal island), and then evolved within the Marine/Navy fighter squadrons during the desperate WWII battle for Guadalcanal and the Pacific Theatre game changer at the Battle Of Midway.

1954 MAKING A MARINE PILOT WARRIOR

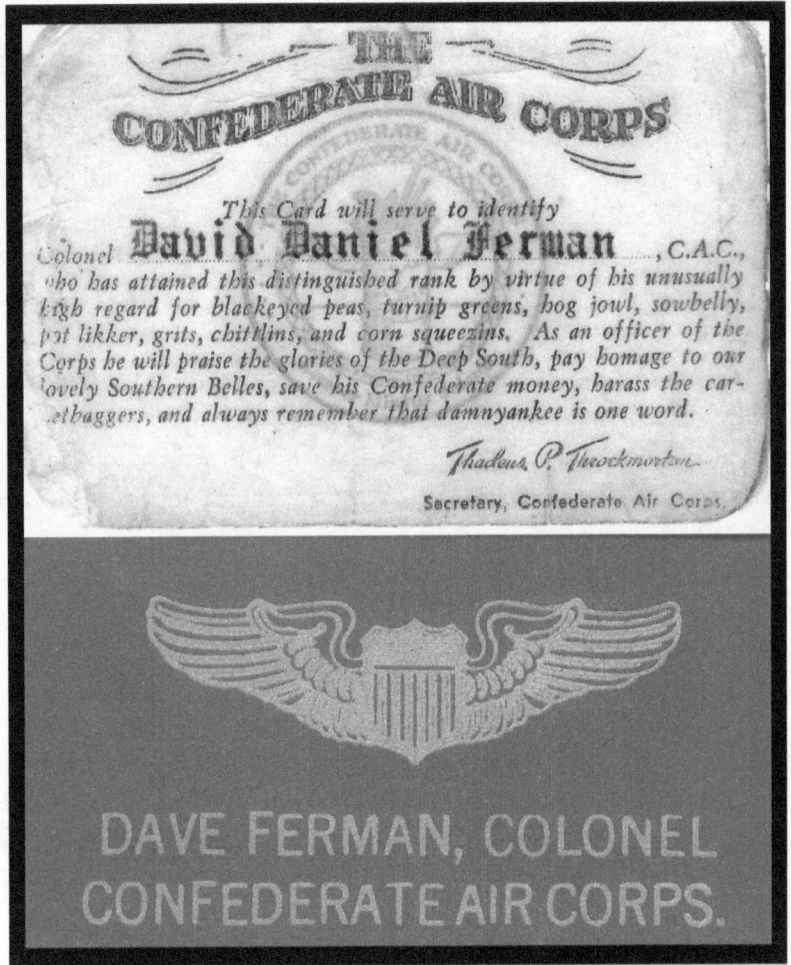

Figure 11. Confederate Air Corps Induction

Take my word for it, that was not a hollow ceremonial honor. The perks were many and plenty. As a full-fledged member of the storied CAC, I gained incredible status and acceptance with all of the CAC Naval Aviators in the Training Command, including some of the instructors and the Admiral as well. All CAC pilots were designated as colonels, no matter what their current ranks in the U.S. Navy or Marines, and all were absolutely equal within the CAC. And thanks to my open gate perk as the Cadet Battalion High Poobah, I became a regular at the raucous monthly CAC midnight T-bone steak and keg parties which began long after the other NavCads were tucked into their bunks for the night. At several meetings, I believe that I was the only CAC pilot present who had not shot down at least one Japanese aircraft.

All of those perks were incredibly entertaining, but I also darned near killed myself in a fluke crash that probably would not have happened like it did if the NAS Sauffley Field Safety Officer had not been a fellow CAC colonel and a very good friend as well. I'll tell you about that later in the normal order of things.

Although my Dad was the Editorial Cartoonist for the Wichita Beacon newspaper—it was the only local competition for Murdock's Wichita Eagle newspaper—I had a very warm feeling for the Eagle until years later when Murdock bought the Wichita Beacon, and his cruddy personnel pukes laid off my Dad. Would you care to read some dirty words? Okay, maybe another time.

18. ARAPAHO WAR CRY

Among the perks of being the Cadet Battalion Commander was a private suite of rooms instead of the usual dual arrangement with two NavCads to a barracks room. I had not only a private bedroom, but also a private study and meeting room, my private telephone, and my own bathroom. In my private potty, I had my very own shower, which eventually led to a really silly misnomer.

With all of that privacy, few ever saw my white derriere, so they apparently thought that I was deeply tanned all over. Ergo, darned near everyone in the NavCad battalion and not just a few of the instructors were sure that I was an American Indian because I was so deeply tanned. No matter how much I denied that silly gossip, most of the NavCads and many of the instructors were convinced that I was denying a proud Indian ethnicity. Ridiculous? Of course it was. I had a good tan when I arrived from California, and since I was a son of the beach by choice, I had a darned good tan both summer and winter.

I just loved everything about Pensacola's world-famous white sand beaches and the beach bunny culture, and I could not get enough in a month of Sundays. Therefore, in my uniform, flight suit or swimming gear, I was as brown as a vintage berry so naturally, many believed that included my fanny as well.

Sometimes, a bunch of us NavCads would pool our minimal finances and rent a beach house or three for the weekend. Often these clapboard shacks were almost as sandy inside as outside, but the beer was always cold so complaints were few and far between. We had our own food, bunks, potties, showers, refrigerators, screened front porches and all of the other essentials for delightful weekends on those beautiful white sandy beaches.

During the day, we would compete to see who could pick-up the best looking girls; the genuine keepers. That morphed into our competition for the best and the worst pickup lines. I think that I won the worst pickup line when I snagged one of the better-looking beach bunnies of the season with a note delivered on the beach by a really cute little guy about four years old; another future son of the beach no doubt. It read: "Do you like apples? I like apples."

My buddies thought that was the most inept opening line they had ever heard (and so did I), but bingo, for some inexplicable reason, Trish and I mutually hit it off as good as any and better than most. Stupid? Heck yes that was a stupid pickup line, but it worked. In the Marines, we have a saying: "If it's stupid but it works; it ain't stupid."

Of course, I thought that Trish was a great catch for so many reasons. She was bright eyed, funny, smart, stacked and a good smooch for a first (and last) moonlit date on the beach. Also, one of my guys commented that if Moses had seen Trish in her teeny weenie bikini, there would have been no sixth commandment. I thought that was a bit much, but to each his own.

Unfortunately, Trish was a passing tourist from one of the Seven Sisters Colleges way back in the northeast, and I never saw or heard from her again. Some believe that time makes the heart grow fonder. However, huge distances bring a shot of reality into any such equation. Like they say in downtown France: "Aw revolver, murky bucket, Chevrolet coupe', pie ala mode" or something like that. Kapesh?

After trolling for the elusive best beach bunnies all day, we often partied around a fairly substantial bon fire on the beach or just inland from the white sandy beaches in the white sandy dunes. No matter how many babes we started with, we ended up with a lot more as our bon fire became a tempting beacon for darned near every pretty party pal on the beach. We never discriminated. Any and all beach bunnies were welcome. Marine NavCads were funny that way. We all went for great looking gals who frolicked and fooled around on Pensacola's white sandy beaches.

Oh yeah, back to my really snazzy, year-around tan. Well, one evening my buddy RUT Temple got tired of me denying my Indian ethnicity about the same time that I got tired of denying that stupid gossip. To finally put an end to the incessant nagging, tongue in cheek, I admitted that I was indeed an Arapaho Indian Warrior from the Great Plains of southern Kansas, Oklahoma and Texas. And since the guys and gals around the bon fire that night so willingly accepted that heaping crock of malarkey, I went a step further and made up the screeching, high pitched Arapaho war cry which phonetically sounded something like: "Iiiiiiiieeeeeeeebahhhhh! Hoooeeeee. Hoooeeeeee" (as in BS being a lot of hooey).

In the deep, dark shadows of the moon-swept sand dunes around a beautiful Florida beach in the dead of night, the fearsome Arapaho war cry reverberated like a primitive howl of defiance and/or victory over anything that this too fickle world could throw at this brown skinned warrior. It worked for me, so I kept it in my repertoire for special occasions like New Year's night and the births of all three of our children. Multiple shotgun blasts and/or cherry bombs are just too darned much, especially when a bunch of cop cars are cruising our neighborhood.

19. DEBUTANT "GOOD GIRLS"

One fine morning, former Marine Cpl., NavCad Jerry F. was highly peeved at all women for some darned reason. I could not understand that because my mother was a woman, and my little sister would be one within a few years. Anyway, Jerry swore that he was going to be a hermit and never wanted to date any woman ever again. It seems that several local gals had spirited him away from the party, but then grossly chided him about what he could not do that which they could do all night, or something like that.

Our consensus answer to that quandary was to bring in a proper, debutante, "good girl" from Mobile, Alabama's high society to show Jerry that not all women were like those gross local trailer-trash gals like those with whom he had been frolicking. We figured that such a fine young southern belle would be sure to modify his new unsociable attitude.

That "good girl" showed up the following weekend at our NavCad formal ball at the Officers' Club, after which we all adjourned to a very nice beach party to cap a wonderful summer evening. Much later, while answering Nature's nagging call, I almost stumbled over Jerry and the "good girl" debutante lying snockered on a beach towel deep in the moon-swept sand dunes. He was wearing only a sand encrusted towel, dry heaving and too darned snockered to do anything but moan pitifully.

Also down to one half of the skimpiest bikini swimming suit that I had ever seen, a vision of lovely lustfulness in the moonlight, Jerry's "good girl" date from Mobile was very busy but unsuccessfully trying to do anything and everything that she could do to get back to whatever she had on her mind for their first and last date with Jerry.

The next morning, Jerry's bad attitude about all young women was alive and thriving again. Like a wise man once said: "the best laid plans of NavCads and high-society debutantes often go astray."

However, as they often say in my native Wabash Land near downtown Wichita, Kansas: "That'll learn ya', durn ya'."

20. JUNKER SNJS

With those junky old outdated SNJs, accidents and fatalities became so common that year that our fragile mortality too often cluttered our minds. The thing was, those fatalities always seemed to happen in groups of three, so every NavCad was on pins and needles after a second fatality happened in a sequence, and stayed at a pretty high level of jitters until the third fatality was over and done with. Then, almost everyone relaxed, maybe too much, until the next fatality.

In 12 consecutive months in 1954 and 1955, I believe we had at least a dozen fatal accidents in the Pensacola Training Command involving an unknown number of NavCads and instructor pilots. Unfortunately, the usual attitude was like: "That poor devil, but better him than me." That was a lousy attitude, but under the stressful conditions at that time, it was not surprising. With those old SNJ junkers, destiny seemed to be found at the luck of the draw.

One afternoon, I was going out on the flight line trying to find my assigned aircraft, and I heard a loud bang overhead and to the west. Looking up, I saw a ball of black smoke, and then two burning aircraft falling separately to earth. But again, just like at our graduation ceremony from ground school, there was only one parachute to be seen as the wreckage fell into the dense wetlands along the shore.

As usual, we continued flight operations uninterrupted, and that evening during supper, somebody passed the word about the identity of the dead pilots. I hardly knew either guy, but as was our custom at that time, we went over to the Cadet Club, toasted their memory for an hour or so, and then did not mention their names again as far as I know.

21. JUST ANOTHER DAY AT WORK

We were flying a two-plane formation (figure 12) trying to work out some rough spots when Bob, my usual wingman at that time, experienced some kind of a minor explosion in his engine compartment, which blew his entire cowling off and sprayed oil all over his windshield. As cool as any pro and without asking for an emergency approach, Bob landed his SNJ using the standard race-track pattern by skidding it somewhat sideways on his final approach so that he could see around the blackened windscreen while I flew on his tail in the same landing pattern and talked him through the landing pattern. Later, Marine NavCad George Baumerman had the exact same thing happen, and he brought his little SNJ junker home the same way as well. Things like that happened so often that parts being shivered off those old junkers was hardly worth mentioning. That sounds crazy, but that is a fact.

Figure 12. Two-Plane Formation

After landing, Bob jacked his seat up to the highest level, looked over the top of the windscreen, and taxied his aircraft back to the flight line like as if nothing unusual had happened. After debriefing and filling out the squawk sheet on his aircraft, Bob and I walked over to the Cadet Club and got completely sloshed. Like they say, "Any excuse in a storm."

22. ENSIGN "KNOW-IT-ALL" BLEW HIS AVIATION CAREER

The cocky young Annapolis-graduate ensign apparently considered himself to be an expert on just about anything and everything. After a couple of serious demonstrations, he was not going to be told one darned thing about how to bail out of an airplane. At the bailout trainer, we had a complete SNJ aircraft raised on two 8-inch diameter metal poles with a bit larger than standard propeller that somewhat simulated the airflow over the cockpit during a bailout at altitude. A bent, two-part trampoline (one section horizontal and a second/trailing section at something like a 45-degree angle behind the horizontal section) was aligned just below the aircraft to catch the students after they jumped.

The standard procedure to bail out of an SNJ was to crouch in the cockpit facing the starboard side while keeping out of the wind stream, and then jump out much like a low dive in a swimming competition while trying to jam our noses against the trailing edge of the wing. However, the cadet's nose would never come close to the trailing edge of the wing because the high-speed airflow from the propeller would push the jumper between the wing and the tail assembly, and in perfect form to land safely in the bent two-section trampoline without getting too scuffed in the process.

I really enjoyed that exercise and I jumped several times just for the pure fun of it. In fact, they took my picture jumping out of the trainer for a revised NavCad brochure. If you can find the 1954 version, that's me. The know-it-all ensign, however, knew better than to jump with his nose aimed at the trailing edge of the wing as well demonstrated and precisely instructed. Instead, he jumped high to avoid the trailing edge of the wing, the airflow caught him, tumbled him violently and uncontrollably splayed out while he was in the air, and he broke his neck when he hit the trampoline as wrong as wrong could be. We think that he may have recovered okay eventually, but we never saw him again. But heck, he could be a retired admiral by now so I won't mention his name.

23. NAVCAD "GOT BUCK$"

Gracious, I almost forgot about NavCad Freddy something or other back at NAS Whiting fairly soon after we began flight training. I did not have a car and NAS Whiting was way out in the boonies about 20 miles east of Pensacola. Therefore, I had to hitch hike with other NavCads and Navy personnel who drove back and forth every day. There was a lot of Whiting-to-Pensacola and back traffic, so hitch hiking on liberty was no big deal. There was always someone going my way whether coming or going.

Freddy was a quiet little guy who didn't talk much, but was getting along pretty well as he developed in the natural progression from NavCad to Naval Aviator. I never flew with him, but I heard that he did okay for a college guy. In fact, I don't believe that there was anything unusual about Freddy for the first couple of weeks after his first solo flight until one evening after all flight operations were done for the day, he picked up another NavCad and myself at the main gate, but not in his old 1939 four-door Chevy. Instead, he was driving a brand new, tricked-out Lincoln Continental that had all of the bells, whistles and chrome imaginable and then some more for good measure.

According to Freddy, his most favorite grandma had just died while he was in flight school, and had left something more than a million dollars cash free and clear just for him. Remember, this was 1954 when a million dollars was a heck of a lot of money. That was something like maybe six or eight million dollars in today's money, or maybe even more. Who knows? That's above my pay grade.

Anyway, all that money had apparently affected him more than somewhat, because as we drove down a long two-lane blacktop back road toward the main east to west highway to Pensacola, Freddy saw the lights of another car just turning onto the back road a heck of a long way behind us, and he went all Able Sugar, yelled: "They're after me," and put his foot into the carburetor.

I am here to tell you that the large and luxurious 1954 Lincoln Continental was a surprisingly fast car, and in the hands of young ex-four-door Chevy driver who had probably never driven faster than 60 mph or so in his entire life, we had a fanny puckering ride all of the way into Pensacola. In fact, neither of us hitch hikers even mentioned getting back together with Freddy when it was time to return to the base that night.

Several days later, I heard that Freddy drove into downtown Pensacola wearing his flight suit, flight jacket, Mae West and flying helmet (an absolute No No) to impress the ladies. However, the first Shore Patrol that saw him getting out of his car put him in their car and ruined his whole evening. Needless to say, we never saw ol' Freddy again. In fact, we heard that he got a Section 8 (a ticket to the funny farm) discharge, and was sent home to wallow in unimaginable luxury with no more military service commitment.

Sometimes I wonder who was messing around with who? Way to go Freddy. Like they say: "Ya' gotta' get it while the getting is good, so good, so good."

24. "HOUKAH HEI:" A GOOD DAY TO DIE

The Flight Safety Officer was out of pocket again, when a huge, black squall line approached rapidly from the west by northwest. Unfortunately, flight operations could not be cancelled without the Safety Officer's specific approval. As I pre-flighted then warmed up my aircraft, a solid wall of black cloud clear down to the ground could be seen approaching the north end of the runway. I called the control tower and asked for the field's flight status. Surprisingly, it was still A-okay for both dual and solo flights although anyone could see that flight operations should have already been cancelled for a while. I believe that I called the tower one more time as I taxied off the parking line, and again as I lined up on the south end of the generally north/south runway with the black, threatening squall line firmly in place on the north end of the runway and coming on like gangbusters.

Apparently, there was still no Safety Officer available to cancel flight operations. So I figured to heck with it, said "Hookah hei" (which I believe is Lakota Sioux for "This is a good day to die") into my microphone, and added power to takeoff. Just as my wheels lifted off the runway, I flew into that black wall and could see nothing but the inside of my windshield and my instruments. Barely able to hold altitude or a straight and level attitude in the extreme turbulence at such a low altitude, I sucked up my wheels and continued as level as I could hold it for several miles until I remembered the very tall radio tower dead ahead.

As I zigged hard to the left, through the blackness I saw the flashes of the tower strobe lights where I could have zagged to the right. Then, as I finally pulled up and out of the black squall line into the bright sunshine above, the Safety Officer finally cancelled all flight operations. Better late than...aw forget it.

Several of us solo NavCads could have easily bought the farm. Holy Joe, my overworked guardian angel, definitely earned his flight pay that day.

25. NAVCAD LEON DYKUS

My good buddy, NavCad Leon Dykus, another Marine corporal, was already celebrating with a pitcher half full of Budweiser in the Cadet Club when I arrived just after supper. Dykus said that he was the daddy of a fine new baby Marine. That was quite a surprise because Marine NavCads could not be married, let alone the new father of a future Marine Commandant.

According to his story, Dykus had stopped at his home town for a surprise visit of his girlfriend on his way to the Pensacola Training Command. Unfortunately, his long-time honey did not know that he would arrive that day, so she was out on the town with her friends or somebody like that. Anyway, when Dykus showed up at his sweetie's front door for a surprise date that evening, she was not there. However, her cute little sister was. So what the heck, Dykus and the little sister went out on the town just to pass the time away, they got kind of crazy and painted the town Marine green, and they had the first of many great times.

Long story short, Dykus swapped sisters, they had a whirlwind romance, and they were married before he left town on the way to Pensacola. The rules being what they were, Dykus did not say boo doodly about his newly marital status when he checked in at Pensacola. In fact, he did not say anything to anybody including yours truly until that same evening in the Cadet Club.

Naturally, Dykus and I spent the evening toasting his little future Marine baby son. After the Cadet Club closed, I borrowed somebody's car (I didn't know whose car it was, but the keys were on the seat) and used my Cadet Battalion Commander all-day every-day gate pass to go get a couple of fifths of Old Tanglefoot. Then we stayed up almost all night celebrating how baby Leon Dykus Jr. would take his first steps at a 30-inch pace and 90 steps per minute while we finished off both bottles with the help of some of the other Marine cadets that we rousted out of their racks to celebrate the happy occasion. Good Tanglefoot beats cigars every time.

The next morning, I was out on the flight line looking for my assigned airplane, but I could not find it even though all of the aircraft were parked in the order of their call (ID) numbers, which were also painted large on both sides of their fuselages and on their vertical stabilizers.

After a while, I bumped into Dykus, and darned if he could find his airplane either. So we followed the course of least resistance and both of us reported to the base sickbay.

As I told the doctor: "I have a terrible headache. My stomach is puke sick, and I can barely stand up. In fact, Doc, this is the worst danged hangover that I have ever had." The doctor was amazed. He said that was the first time a NavCad had ever admitted that he could not fly because he was too darned hung over to even find his airplane. As a reward for my unusual honesty, he grounded me for the rest of the day, and gave me a chit to go back to the barracks and sleep it off. As I turned to walk away, Dykus got only as far as the doctor's office door. He leaned against it to steady himself, pointed at me and said: "Same as him. Same as him."

That was about 64 years ago, so I have stopped checking the list of senior Marine officer promotions to see if Dykus Jr. lived up to his daddy's expectations. I hope so. His daddy was a darned good Marine.

26. RUT'S HIGH SOCIETY WEDDING

Remember Marine Cpl/NavCad Richard Temple (RUT), a good friend and former USMC rifle coach when I was a DI at MCRD Sam Diego? Somehow, he became engaged to Pi Melon, an uber socialite from New York City. She visited Pensacola several times, but since I was an oblivious dummy from the endless dirt plains of Kansas, I was too busy with other unimportant things, and turned down a double date with her female companion (or maybe that was her sister).

When they were married after RUT earned his Navy Wings of Gold, I heard that RUT's new father-in-law gave him the New York City-to-New Jersey helicopter airline. The new in-laws were THE Melons. It could not happen to a better guy. Good luck, RUT. Semper fi.

27. LESSONS LEARNED IN BOXING CLASS

My good buddy since DI School, Joe D. Bolling and I looked like two peas in a pod to a lot of people. We were constantly mistaken for each other because we were the same height, weight and coloring, and we both got out of duty occasionally in the Marines by being three-sport jocks on top of everything else.

Every NavCad had to take a boxing class instructed by a mouthy, irritating Annapolis-graduate Lt.jg who proclaimed that he had been an extraordinary boxer at Annapolis or some horse hockey like that. Since Joe D. and I were the only heavyweights in the class, we were matched to practice boxing with each other. However, since neither of us felt like punching out a good buddy, we danced around and clinched and fooled around, and chuckled a lot during the entire first round of our match.

Understandably, the instructor watching us got all bent out of shape. I could not blame him. However, this bozo became verbally abusive about Joe D. and me loafing like that. I vaguely remember him saying "you girls" a couple of times, as well as some other derogatory terms that did not sit well with either of Joe D. or myself. However, he then made the really big mistake of singling me out, and choosing to show me and the class how it should be done in the boxing ring.

As he was preparing to show me how to box, I casually mentioned to him that I was a bit bigger than him so maybe he shouldn't climb into the boxing ring with me, and maybe he should pick someone his own size for his demonstration. Sadly for him, he ignored my advice. You talk about an alligator mouth and tadpole fanny.

I don't think that bozo had ever boxed a left hander before because he looked really surprised when I jumpstarted the festivities by hitting him on his nose with three or four quick right jabs that brought tears to his eyes. Then I popped him a left uppercut to his gut that brought his hands down just before he deftly blocked my overhand left with his face and then sat down abruptly on the deck.

Joe D., who volunteered to be the NavCad referee, helped him get up like any gentleman boxing student should, and commented: "Go get him, Sir. He can't do that to you." But I did, and that time he sat down on the deck again, but a lot sooner. However, that time he stayed down. "Good thinking, Sir," Joe D. said as my boxing lesson came to an early conclusion. I was hoping that it would last a little longer.

I have to admit that was one of the very few times that I really enjoyed whittling down a very surprised, big mouthed, irritating, elitist Ivy League clown who was probably more qualified to teach an etiquette class than a boxing class.

The following week, we had a new boxing instructor who was a lot more qualified to teach a boxing class. That first instructor must have been darned embarrassed when the word got around the "O" Club that I had decked him twice during the first and only round of the three-round demonstration match. Some people should never make corporal, let alone lieutenant jg. Like the song goes: "Here's a quarter, call someone who cares."

28. FOUL FRENCH CADETS

I had about a dozen French cadets directly under my command. All had graduated from the French Naval Academy and had volunteered for flight training in the United States. These guys answered to me, but they had a French liaison officer who pretty much served as their "yes man." I don't speak French and they would not admit that they knew much English except "mail call," "chow call," and "liberty call" although we all knew that all of their instructions while flying in our aircraft were spoken in English. Of course, it helped to learn several dozen commands and cuss words in French. That finished off the "Ne parle Englese" foolishness.

The bigger problem with the French cadets in the summer was that they never took a shower no matter how hot and sweaty our unair-conditioned wooden barracks were, and they didn't even send their dirty laundry to the cleaners like every other cadet did very frequently. In fact, believe it or not, they would take a dirty, sweaty khaki uniform, roll it up tightly and precisely, tie the roll with a cord, and then toss that roll into their chest of drawers. When they had gone through all of their French cadet uniforms and their French naval academy uniforms, they would then take out the rolled up uniform that had been tied up first, untie it, shake it out and then wear it again. I kid you not.

I finally had to put them in the far end of a wing of the barracks that was separate from the American cadets. Their rooms were located at the end of a separate hall, but we needed a wall. In a word, they stunk to high heaven. None of the other cadets wanted to be billeted near them.

Their only saving grace was that every one of them spent Saturdays and Sundays on the beautiful white sands of Pensacola Beach chasing women in their comically brief Speedo swimming suits. So instead of their one weekly swimming lesson in the base pool on Wednesdays, I convinced the base C.O. to add a second swimming lesson for them and rescheduled those events to Tuesday and Thursday. That way, they were in the water up to their giblets every other day, and Mondays became their official weekly trip-to-the-cleaners days with no exceptions acceptable.

There is more than one way to skin a frog.

29. LEARN FROM ACCIDENT REPORTS

The formal aviation accident reports were full of valuable information, and we read each one as soon as it was published so we could learn what to look for and what to avoid. Naval aviation accident reports were usually extremely detailed. They contained very precise and meticulous biddyfuzz information such as: "I flew over Pensacola Beach at 2 minutes and 27 seconds after noon, and there were 52 red bikinis and 27 blue bikinis…blah, blah, blah." and other minutia like that for page after page after page. Well, they weren't all quite that nit picking, but you get the picture.

However, one French cadet was more succinct than usual. He had complained that he did not want to fly that day, but was commanded to take a solo flight by his instructor, and he subsequently crashed while landing. In his accident report he wrote: "If I had not flown today, I would not have had an accident." That was his whole and entire statement after destroying an expensive and irreplaceable U.S. Navy aircraft.

In another accident report, an American NavCad wrote: "When I read 'Hamilton Hydromantic' on my propeller, I knew that my engine had stopped." No joke. Another NavCad wrote that when his airplane suddenly rolled straight forward end over end 360 degrees several times, he saw his entire tail assembly tumbling away behind him. Therefore, he "believed" that the following airplane in that multi-plane formation "may have" overridden him and severed his tail assembly with its propeller.

Another took several thousand words to essentially say that he had ran out of airspeed, altitude and ideas, all at the same time. We often mined a lot of laughs out of those otherwise serious accident reports.

Obviously, some of those self-styled aviation geniuses could not pour pee out of a boot unless instructions were printed plainly on that boot's heel.

Then there was the classic when another NavCad almost landed on an LSO (Landing Signal Officer) controlled secondary airfield with his wheels up. As he approached very close to landing, the LSO called the NavCad on the radio and told him that his landing gear was not down. But the plane kept coming at him with its landing gear still up, so the LSO fired his Very Pistol (smoke flare) straight up into the air. However, the airplane still continued coming at the LSO in the landing pattern.

Finally, the LSO fired his second Very Pistol directly at the airplane, and the flare actually bounced off the NavCad's windshield. Only then did the NavCad get the message and break off his landing. Afterward, when the LSO debriefed that NavCad in no uncertain terms, the NavCad said that the horn (which indicates that the wheels are still up when they should be down) was blaring so loud he could not hear the LSO's verbal commands to lower his landing gear.

I will swear on a stack of bibles yea high, nobody could make up some of this stuff.

30. A FIRST-CLASS 1ST CLASS SAILOR

One evening, my NavCad buddy Dick Welch—a walking, talking junk yard dog who we called "Firecracker" because he could go from placid to fist fighting in an instant—and I were taking it easy in a semi-sleezy country/western bar just north of Pensacola while hoping to finally meet the Girl Of My Dreams. After I put a quarter into the juke box and picked three records, I sat down at a table when a five-stripe sailor (he was a something-or-other first class) at the next table began singing along with my favorite record. So I told him that I had paid all of that money to hear those songs, and I did not appreciate him drowning out the lyrics with his lousy off-key howling. Of course, he told me what I could do with that. So I stood up, and he stood up bigger.

Naturally, this led to that, and that led to the other, and pretty soon he took a poke at me, I blocked it with my right arm and popped him with my best left hand square on his kisser. But surprise, surprise, he did not sit down on the deck like I expected. About that time, a bunch of sailors, a few NavCads led by my buddy Firecracker Welch and some civilians were pushing and shoving and smacking each other around while the swabby song bird and I traded a couple more pretty good punches with not much to show for it.

Very soon, a Navy Shore Patrol, which must have been parked outside, came busting through the front door blowing their whistles and rounding up the troublemakers. Looking for cover, I could see no way out when that Navy song bird shoved a Coke Cola in front of me and we sat at that table drinking Cokes and talking to each other like old friends while the SPs rounded up about a dozen troublemakers and herded them out of the building and probably off to the brig to cool down.

I was impressed. So I put another quarter in the jukebox, and allowed as how that sailor could sing along if he darned well wanted to sing along. He did, and pretty soon we did. Surprisingly, he and I sounded a lot better with our two-part harmony. It wasn't like singing with George Jones, but that was a darned good song and we did the best that we could. Anyway, I have always been partial to guys who think fast on their feet; even sailors. Some of those guys are truly salty, particularly when under a lot of pressure from Shore Patrols.

31. FATAL TAKEOFF CRASH

A bunch of us NavCads were coming back to the flight-line hangar after lunch when we saw a fatal crash not 60 yards away. On his very first flight, just after lifting off the ground, a college-graduate NavCad panicked, and pulled straight back on the flight control ("joy") stick. The aircraft momentarily went straight up, quickly stalled, swapped ends, fell nose down near the end of the runway, exploded, and then burned.

When we got there, the entire engine forward of the lord mounts was doubled back into the front cockpit, although the rear cockpit was hardly damaged. The cadet's right hand was cut off at his wrist by the propeller and his face was smashed horribly by the impact. However, he was still twitching so we tried to pull him out of the wreckage in case of an explosion as his instructor wandered around incoherently babbling in a thin sheet of flaming gasoline on the runway.

At his funeral, his parents were terribly bent out of shape with the military, and they would not allow even a military honor guard. What did they think flight training was: some kind of a picnic in the park?

When you live by the art of war, you can sometimes die by the art of war. Nuff said.

32. PRINCIPLES-OF-FLIGHT CLASS

In the Principles-of-Flight class, I understood the characteristics of the laminar flow wing in flight, but was having a hard time applying that principle to a particular problem with an inverted wing in a flat spin. I was sitting in the front row of the class room, lost in thought, when our instructor, a Navy lieutenant and fellow Confederate Air Corps member, asked me in a hesitant, concerned manner: "What's the matter, Dave?" Jerked out of my mental search for the answer and dragged into the here and now, I told him that nothing was the matter; I was just thinking. He replied: "Don't do that Dave; you're scaring me."

33. THE USUAL "UNUSUAL ATTITUDES"

All alone in a hot little airplane anywhere between 5,000 and 10,000 feet of altitude (and sometimes a little bit higher or lower), aerial acrobatics are the most fun that you can have with your clothes on. Besides that, acrobatics lead to "unusual attitudes" training while under an opaque hood to simulate violent changes in aircraft attitudes after dark with no visual orientation outside the aircraft. That is a good thing to know if you plan on making Naval Aviation your career.

On my first such flight, Lt. Paul Stretch closed my hood in the front seat so that I could not see outside the aircraft, did a series of really violent snap rolls, split "S's", stalls and other disorienting maneuvers, then turned the plane over to me while inverted with my wheels down and full flaps at an altitude of about 9,000 feet. Of course, the first thing I did was lean down to pull up my wheels and move the control to zero flaps, which tricked me into inadvertently putting foreword pressure on the joy stick, and that popped us into an inverted split "S" dive that almost red-lined our airspeed while we fell straight down like a rock for several thousand feet.

Despite the little SNJ howling like a homesick banshee, I still did not know where the heck I was until Lt. Stretch told me to look at my altimeter ("dammit!"), which was unwinding like a yoyo. I was diving inverted on my back, but so disoriented by all of Lt. Stretch's preconditioning that I could not feel the pull of gravity and the artificial horizon instrument was caged. So I did a half of a slow roll like a basackwards split "S" to get the aircraft out of inverted flight and then added back stick and neutral rudder so that we finally recovered, but well below the bailout altitude of 5,000 feet. I had blown my first unusual attitudes test, but I fully recovered from the next two exercises so that it was not a bad day after all.

Afterward, while we were walking back to the hangar from the flight line, Lt. Stretch told me that he had tried to take the joystick away from me in the middle of that first unusual attitude test, but that I had taken it away from him. He was really bent out of shape because we had that problem once before, and he had instructed me to always fly with just two fingers around the joystick. He believed that I obviously had not done that.

I protested that I was flying with just two fingers on the joystick just like he had told me to do. Lt. Stretch stopped walking, looked up at me rather slowly like the father of a new date, and he said through tight jaws: "Ferman, you're just too damned big. From now on, I want you to fly with just one finger on the control stick." What could I say? "Aye aye, Sir!" which means that "I hear you and I will obey you." And I did.

That may be why the middle finger on my right hand may be a little bigger than my other fingers. I have heard worse explanations why a middle finger could be so often displayed, but this one, for a change, is abso-danged-posolutely, 99, 44, 100 percent true.

34. AIR-TO-AIR COMBAT WAS FINALLY FUN.

After finishing the acrobatics and unusual attitudes tests, I was ready to be introduced to the art of air-to-air combat: i.e., WWII style, one-on-one dog fighting. Lt. Stretch's pre-flight instructions were incredibly cryptic: "I'll meet you over Spanish Fort at 10,000 feet." That was it; nothing more.

When I arrived at our rendezvous site, Lt. Stretch was at 9,000 feet rather than 10,000 feet when he radioed me. His detailed orientation lecture was: "You have a 1,000-foot advantage. Let's get it on."

Lt. Stretch had been a Navy fighter pilot during the Korean War, and he probably saw action in WWII (I never saw his ribbons), so he had quite an advantage over any new cadet. Every time we tangled, whether I had the 1,000-foot altitude advantage or he had the altitude advantage, whether we started in parallel directions or opposite directions, the result was always the same. He won. I lost. I tried half-loop Immelman inverted changes of direction, Split "S" dives, barrel rolls, consecutive snap rolls, everything in my repertoire including spins and hammerhead stalls. It made no difference. No matter what I did, at the end of the fight he would be glued to my tail and would gleefully chortle: "Bup, bup, bup, I just shot you down, cadet. I just killed you."

Whether baseball, tennis, table tennis or aviation dog fighting, I always liked to learn by competing with someone better than me. But after several strings of absolute defeats one after another, I was getting pretty darned tired of Lt. Stretch's constant crowing in the air and during debriefing after the flight. But he did not know that I knew what to do with the resources available to me.

Outside of one-on-one flight instruction, one of the best sources of information on anything to do with flying was the main Officer's ("O") Club at NAS Pensacola. And one of the best sources within the O Club was a Marine aviator, Captain Fisher who had flown with Pappy Boyington's Black Sheep Squadron in the Cactus Air Corps during the battle for Guadalcanal and thereafter. As one of the original members of the Confederate Air Corps in support of probably the newest member of the Confederate Air Corps, he was more than happy to give me the information that I needed to win at least one dog fight.

Those lessons only cost me the price of a few discounted mixed drinks and a couple of missed hours of sleep as he and I closed the bar and were the last guys out the door before the O Club closed for the night. However, by that time, I was finally ready to kick Lt. Paul Stretch's donkey, and I could not wait to clobber him.

The next afternoon, Lt. Stretch and I met at 9,000 feet over Spanish Fort, Alabama. I forget who had the 1,000-foot advantage, but it did not make much difference because very soon we were both at the same altitude and Lt. Stretch was closing behind me in a little tighter left turn than I could safely hold without stalling. He was sure to catch up in a minute, and once again I would be toast. At least, that's what he was probably thinking. At least, I was hoping that he was in that mindset.

That is when I snapped into a tight right turn, Lt. Stretch again went into a tighter turn that put him behind me a couple of hundred feet but slightly to the right of my precise line of flight just like Captain Jack had told me. So I dumped my nose a lot as if to begin a terminal dive, and as Lt. Stretch began to follow me just a heartbeat later, I pulled straight back, firewalled the manifold pressure, tickled the rpm, and went straight up like a homesick angel.

Since we were flying identical aircraft with identical capabilities and limitations, my slightly longer dive (about a second or so) and earlier application of "firewall manifold pressure" gave me a little more airspeed for transition into my straight up climb. "Many 'littles' do indeed make a 'much'." So although Lt. Stretch was essentially just a little to the right of being on my tail for a kill, he had just a touch less air speed when he determined that I was leading him into a hammerhead stall where my aircraft would go straight up vertically until it could no longer climb. If that maneuver continued to its climax, my plane would then hang on its propeller for just an instant, then start to actually back straight down vertically before the front end would slam down hard as it stalled, and then the little SNJ would swap ends into a dive. That was pretty much the norm.

Close on my tail but still not on my exact line of flight for a good shot, Lt. Stretch could see that hammerhead developing, and he knew he was in danger of me backing down and possibly slamming down onto him if I wasn't on the ball. So he kicked his right rudder and peeled off to the side away from my stall. As I saw him start to peel off, just before stalling, I kicked the right rudder hard with full right control stick, and peeled off right on his tail while he did not have enough airspeed or air flow over his control surfaces to pull one of his fancy "old pilots/bold pilots" tricks.

In an instant, I glued myself dead nuts on his tail at something far less than 50 yards and yelled into the mike: "Bang, bang, bang! I just shot you down! Sir. You…are…DEAD, Sir!"

Back on the ground, Lt. Stretch complained through tight jaws that I had broken through the artificial hard pan (i.e., substitute ground level) at 5,000 feet during my celebratory diving victory roll, but that made no difference. I had won a dogfight against a very good Naval Aviator, and it made my day. It still does. However, Lt. Stretch then won our last two dog fights handily but he didn't cackle quite as much as before.

35. CAPTAIN FISHER FROM THE BLACK SHEEP SQUADRON

Captain Fisher was an interesting guy and a good friend. I first met him at the Confederate Air Corps midnight beer, beer, beer and T-bone steak parties, and our paths crossed over and over again while both of us were stationed at the Pensacola Training Command. As I mentioned before, he had flown with Pappy Boyington in the famous (infamous?) Black Sheep Squadron, and had shot down several Japanese fighter aircraft, but he was not an ace although he probably should have been.

Captain Fisher had loved to party between missions with Pappy, but he hated to fly as the wingman for Pappy because Pappy had the bad habit of getting on a Jap aircraft's tail, kicking his rudders so that he sprayed the general area side to side until he was flat out of ammunition—the whole nine yards for each machinegun. Then Pappy would head for the barn with Captain Fisher on his wing protecting his giblets. That cut down on Captain Fisher's opportunities to run up his score by a bunch.

A dedicated combat aviator, Captain Fisher decided to be a career Marine pilot, but he was released in 1946 when the Marine Corps had too few front-line fighter aircraft and too many good pilots. So Captain Fisher went home, built a dry cleaning business with three stores and another on the horizon when he was recalled in 1950 for duty in Korea. However, the jet jockeys on both sides took over the dog-fighting business, so Captain Fisher and the other tail-dragger F4U Corsair prop job jockeys did two tours flying close air support for the mud Marines down where you can buy the farm at any time from all of the small arms fire coming up from the ground.

By that time, Captain Fisher's habitually snockered partner back home had bankrupted their business—all three stores were long gone—and Captain Fisher, with something like 11 years of active duty and 4 years in the reserves, once again decided to be a career Marine (a "lifer") since he was more than half way there already. However, once again, with no war to pay the bills for his wife and three little deductions, the Powers That Be decreed that there are old pilots and bold pilots, but there are no old, bold pilots to be retained. So Captain Fisher was faced with the prospect of starting another business from scratch at age 35, although he must stay at the government's beck and call for another 27 years.

Lets see, how old would Captain Fisher be when North Vietnam's General Giap got the urge to take all of South Vietnam? I do hope that Captain Fisher got the benefit of the luck of the draw. To paraphrase future Major General Chesty Puller during the "Banana Wars" in the early 1930s: "It's the only war that we've got."

36. "EVERY DOG HAS HIS DAY"

My flight instructor, Lt. Paul Stretch, had a terrible and well-earned reputation as a hard-to-please instructor and a really hard-nosed check pilot who was satisfied with nothing but perfection. Rumors said that he would give a check-flight "down" (i.e., "failing")grade to the Blue Angels (the Navy/Marine flight demonstration team; the best of the best). Needless to say, I was having a difficult time with Lt. Stretch. Then one Saturday, Lt. Stretch the gun nut, invited me to join him and another Naval Aviator instructor to compete with M1 rifles on the Pensacola Mainside Base's rifle range at 100 and 200 yards because those were the only ranges available. They were sailors and I was a Marine Drill Instructor, so they really didn't have the chance of a snowball in hell. But they didn't know how much they didn't know, so it was a laugher although I kept my giggles to myself, at least at first.

After I soundly kicked both their fannys at both ranges, we were checking our targets one last time when, on a whim I sat up an empty pint whiskey bottle (that we had all been sampling) sideways at 100 yards and let each flight instructor have eight shots at it firing however the heck they were the most comfortable. Neither of them could hit it. So I took one shot at it, noted my M1 loaner rifle hit about two inches to the right of the middle of the bottle. I compensated on my second shot and blew it apart from the standing, offhand stance with a hasty sling. After that, Lt. Stretch became a far-more friendly, helpful instructor.

The moral: there's always a button to punch. You just have to find it and then use it to your best advantage.

37. JIMMY BUFFETT'S DADDY'S MOONSHINE STILL

Just for the heck of it, I began flying practice-gunnery runs on the fishing boats on Mobile Bay, which was not far outside the west end of our designated training area. From about 5,000 feet altitude, I could see a fairly large fishing boat in the deeper channel with a lot of large shapes around and under the water. Then I peeled off and dove on the

1954 MAKING A MARINE PILOT WARRIOR

boat to work on my air-to-ground gunnery techniques. Since I could resist almost anything but temptation, I then shoved my propeller rpm full forward just as I passed over the boat at about redline air speed, which made a loud siren-like noise much like the German Stuka dive bombers during WWII.

That was a hoot, but the dark shapes in the water scattered and the boat crews got more than somewhat irritated. So I began hunting for a new target that would be less likely to file a complaint, although those guys on the boat only had a head-on look at me as I bore sighted them on the way in, and only a pure tail-on look as I headed straight away for the further anonymity of altitude.

A few miles north of Mobile Bay in a dense forest, again a bit outside of our training area, I found some wispy smoke drifting up from a bootlegger's still; but I did not know its origin at that time. That was an even better target because the smoke was more wispy and elusive, and I had to concentrate on it or I would lose it in the forest canopy during the peel-off, steep dive and gunnery run. That target afforded excellent gunnery practice that temporarily overshadowed decent manners and good sense.

I had just made my third or fourth pass on the source of the smoke within a couple of days when I banked sharply and looked straight down through the trees from not much above tree top level where I saw a ragtag bunch of hillbillies down there shaking their rifles at me, and a few were aiming at me although I would only be fully visible to them for a split second.

Fortunately, I wised-up and took the hint so thereafter I usually worked on my gunnery techniques only in the approved areas and approved targets. Also, I would have hated to have to explain bullet holes from an unauthorized training activity in an unauthorized area.

About 38 years later, I met Jimmie Buffett (he's the guy who sings *Marguritaville*) in the Napoleon House Bar at a Writer's Conference in New Orleans, and after an hour or two of sea stories and cold potables, he told me that same whisky still operation north of Mobile Bay was his daddy's, and that the guys on the ground were mui bent because I could have drawn the attention of the local government revenuers who were often hanging around trying to smash a man's prize still and ruin his honest living.

Buffett also remembered that when he was a boy, he had been at his daddy's still in the Alabama woods at the time that I was buzzing it in my obnoxious, noisy little yellow SNJ.

It is, indeed, a very small world.

38. BOOMER THE SAILBOAT NUT

Another of the Confederate Air Corps guys working as flight instructors, Lieutenant Jackson (I think that was his name although he used his squadron nickname of "Boomer"), was an easy going, affable Navy officer who seemed to take almost everything calmly in stride. With his date, he invited me and my date to spend a wonderful holiday plying the clear, blue waters around Pensacola in his 52-foot sailboat from just after breakfast to long after sundown.

Since I was not a sailor, let alone a sailboat sailor, I was a bit apprehensive at first. However, all went well as Boomer told the young ladies and me which ropes to pull, tie or adjust, or whatever and, amazingly, we did just fine all day long. I loved it, and both of our dates were suitably impressed as well. That's always a winner that will get you a second date just about every time.

As we were docking under power under a full moon, I asked Lt. Boomer about his deck, since it was so rough although everything else on that boat was smoothly painted, polished and my idea of truly ship shape. Lt. Boomer told me that the rough deck was for good foot traction when sailing in rough, white-water weather, and that he would call me the very next time we had such conditions so we could go enjoy another cruise under more challenging conditions. Say what?

The very next Sunday morning, the weather was awful and getting worse when the phone in my suite rang. It was Lt. Boomer and he wanted to go get some salty spray on our faces out in the deep blue yonder. At first, I thought that he was kidding me, but he was not. So I lied like a rug, and claimed I had the flu, dysentery, irritable bowel syndrome, the green apple quickstep and anything else that would keep me the heck off that foam-slick deck of that bucking sailing barge that day. And although our first double date had been a definite success, after that I dodged all communications with that wild-eyed white-water fanatic when the sun was not shining.

Looking back, I was in tall cotton. I just did not know it at that time.

39. FIFTY THIRSTY NAVY "ADMIRALS"

A couple of NavCad classes formed a squadron which did a fairly low flyby at the Biloxi, Mississippi Air Force Base (AFB) during the Armed Forced Day Open House, and then formed a tight and precise race-track landing pattern off a simulated carrier break. Each of our planes landed full-stall carrier-style on a 300-foot-long box marked on their humongous 15,000-foot long or longer landing strip. That demonstration was a big hit with a fairly large crowd gathered on the field, and we received a great reception as we taxied up to the grandstand by two's for an overnight visit. Some of their commissioned pilots watched in utter amazement. They probably needed all 15,000 feet to land, and did not fly in formation until well after they received their wings and commissions.

After evening chow, sporting our dress-tan uniforms with shoulder boards, the whole gaggle of NavCads were taken to the Officers' Club by three base buses in a convoy. Since I was the Cadet Battalion Commander, I sat by the front door of the front bus, and as soon as it stopped at the base "O" Club, I hurried inside to beat the rabid mob to the bar. I hate to stand in line when I am thirsty for an adult beverage.

However, when I entered the dining room/bar momentarily by myself, the Air Force officers there saw only the Navy's single "line officer's" star on each of my shoulder boards, and every one of them jumped to attention thinking I was a brigadier general or a one-star admiral even though I didn't look much older than my 21 years.

What the heck could I do; tell them to hush up and sit down? Then, thankfully, 49 more NavCads of all sizes came pouring into the room behind me, each with a single star on his shoulder boards as well. Silently, one by one those officers sat back down sheepishly and tried to explain to their wives and dates why Air Force full colonels and such would render such honors to a young although dapper, left-handed NavCad pilot.

40. THE ADMIRAL'S HAT FIT JUST FINE

It was a dark and stormy night. Well, at least NavCads RUT Temple and I were wearing our rain gear when we arrived at the Officers' Club to wash down a few cold adult beverages after a very long, difficult day. I don't remember if it was actually raining or not, but it doesn't really make a heck of a lot of difference. As was the standard operating procedure (SOP), we checked our uniform rain coats and billed s***-scoop hats with Peaches the hatcheck girl, who flashed each of us big smiles as usual, and a number with which to retrieve our gear when we would be ready to leave the club. During the course of the evening, Marine NavCads George Bailey and George Baummerman joined us, and we had a pleasant and uneventful evening; i.e., nobody scored and nobody got hurt.

Just before closing time, we all went back to the hat-check closet in the lobby, but Peaches had once again danced out the door with some young and eligible Navy officer who obviously did not know what a mistake he was making. That young lady, a vision of healthy loveliness, had a well-earned reputation for fast times and round heels, and she was truly "officers' country" without exception.

Peaches never dated NavCads because no NavCad had enough ready cash, and I was the only NavCad who had the unrestricted gate pass to stay out past midnight during the work week. However, I could not and would not spend the money in the quantities that she desired. Also, I was not interested in catching something that I could regret for the rest of my life.

As a good buddy will often do, RUT took my hat and coat number and retrieved our gear while I finished a sea story with one or both of the Georges. By then, it was raining hard with quite a bit of thunder and lightning. Anyway, RUT slipped my hat on me while I was struggling with pulling my rain coat over my danged shoulder boards. Then, when we stepped outside into the foul weather and the murky darkness of night, several Navy officers saluted me as we passed them. That was initially fairly amusing. But when a couple of full commanders saluted me, I asked RUT why in the heck those officers had saluted me. With casual, laconic humor, RUT replied: "Maybe it's because you're wearing the Admiral's hat."

After that, I always retrieved my own hat whenever Peaches was once again AWOL on another one-night stand.

41. NAVCAD PETE PETERSON OUT-MANEUVERED HIS SHRINK

NavCadet Pete Peterson was a former Navy enlisted man whose combined NavCad and enlisted time equaled the four years for which he had originally committed to the Navy. Therefore, Pete was sure that he was suddenly qualified to be discharged and return to the University of Iowa where he had been a junior majoring in psychology before enlisting in the Navy to avoid the draft.

However, Pete was flying so well that the Navy would not give him his discharge while he was still a NavCad. So Pete decided to fly really bad, get three "downs" from his instructor, get tossed out, and return to school before the next semester began.

On his first intentionally bad flight, Pete's instructor was amazed because Pete was a good pilot. Apologetically he said: "Gee, Pete. I hate to give such a good pilot a 'down,' but that was a truly awful flight and I have no choice." Pete responded: "Wait until you see the next one." Later, Pete confided to me that his next flight was intentionally so bad that he scared himself.

Apparently, a NavCad suddenly not wanting to fly dangerously worn-out airplanes anymore was considered a sign of mental imbalance within the Flight Training Command. Therefore, our base medical doctor sent Pete over to Pensacola Mainside to see a hotshot psychologist several times each week.

Being a Psych major, Pete quickly detected that the shrink at Mainside was using a particular psychological ploy to get Pete to do something that Pete did not want to do. Pete recognized that particular approach from his studies four years earlier at IU.

Unfortunately, Pete could not remember the exact process being used by his shrink, or the best way to scuttle it. So he asked for, and I gave him an open-gate day pass so that he could drive over to the Pensacola Junior College library to find the right psychology books so that he could get up to speed and outmaneuver the dastardly duty shrink. On several occasions when Pete returned from a frustrating session with that shrink, he would hunt through a gaggle of books that he had checked out from the Pensacola Junior College library. When he would finally find the information that he needed to help him to counter his nemesis, he would whoop with joyful anticipation of winning his next mental chess bout with that troublesome shrink.

Outwitting that shrink and getting his discharge had become more of a game than a challenge. Pete Peterson did not like to lose any game, and he was doubly determined not to lose this one.

En guarde, Masseur Navy Shrinkasaurus.

By the way, IU really wanted Pete to come back and finish his major in psychology. They wanted him so badly that as an inducement, IU promised Pete 18 semester hours of credit just for his flight time and Navy experiences. Aaa-danged-mazing! Much later when I attended Wichita State University, I could not negotiate even a single credit hour for my much greater flight time or any of my teaching time as a Marine DI. In fact, WSU would not even give me credit in their dinky one-semester-hour First Aid class in recognition of my intense training and in-the-field experience as a certified USMC DI and First Aid Instructor. Not only that, but they would not give me phys ed. credits for football, basketball, boxing, baseball and DI training activities during my military service.

Like a dummy, I had not initially asked for those credits in advance because for some dumb danged reason after what Pete negotiated at IU, I was sure that was SOP at universities and a done deal. Silly me.

I think it was my granddad, George Volz, the Iowa farmer, who said: "Don't count your chickens before they are hatched." However, Grampa Volz was also the large, hardy, jovial farmer who would take my little third-grader hand in one of his big, work-hardened paws and then grab the cattle-stopping electric fence in his other hand so that I would be good and truly shocked—much more than when I put the tip of the metal screwdriver into the electric outlet by mistake—mostly because Grampa Volz would not let go of me or the electric fence.

I loved Grampa's home-made sausage, playing Tarzan when swinging on ropes in his huge barn and swimming in his horse-watering pond, but after that session with the cattle fence, I kept a safe distance between Gramps and little ol' me.

Like they say: "Fool me once, shame on you. Fool me twice, shame on me. Fool me three times: nevah hoppen, gringo."

42. CHECK FLIGHT SNAFU

After the testing part of my grueling two-hour check flight was completed on everything that we had done before, I was exhausted although I had been flying with just one finger around the joystick just like Lt. Stretch had insisted. My check pilot gave me a thumbs-up and told me to relax. He was going to fly me back to the base from just east of Mobile Bay. So I put my adjustable seat down on the bottom rung, loosed my safety harness so that I could get very comfortable, and I went to sleep in the front seat while the check pilot flew us home from the back seat.

All was sugar plums and lolly pops until, unexpectedly, my check pilot rolled the airplane over to the inverted attitude so that he could look straight down for ducks along the Florida coastline wetlands as I abruptly fell about six inches on my loosened shoulder harnesses and hit my helmet on the inside of the canopy. I was reeling in a galaxy of bright little stars whirling around me, and my neck was hurting as I retightened my safety harness and kept my choice words off our intercom.

Back on the ground, my right arm was not working worth a flip. I could carry my fanny pack parachute under my left arm, but I could not salute, and the flight line hanger was full of Navy/Marine brass. So off we went to the base dispensary where the base flight surgeon listened to my story and then walked around me a couple of times without even touching me. Then he said: "Hummmm," a couple more times, wrinkled his brow, picked up the phone and made me an appointment with the boss shrink at Pensacola Mainside since he thought that the paralysis in my right arm might have a psychological origin.

Say what? I told the flight surgeon that I had just recently overextended my right shoulder when I missed a right jab in a boxing match at the last smoker, and that sudden very sharp jolt in flight had put a hitch in my shoulder's get'along. Never the less, I had to stop by and see the Mainside psychiatrist, the sooner the quicker.

However, in the excitement of leaving early to watch his son's junior high baseball game, somehow that doc forgot to ground me. The next morning my arm was back to normal so I flew five more flights before I could get in to see the psychologist, and be declared not clinically insane as well as formally approved again for solo flights.

At the appointed hour and place, the primo shrink and I talked for the better part of an hour. Finally, he gave me a clean bill of health, but commented that I was just too darned big for the little SNJ aircraft. That poor guy looked so haggard, hungry and unkempt even in his spiffy blue Navy uniform jacket and almost white shirt loosely open below his very noticeable five-o'clock shadow. If I had met him as a stranger in downtown Pensacola, I would have been tempted to buy him a nourishing meal and pay his cab fare home.

So I shook the shrink's hand, bade him to "have a good day" and walked out of his office. However, on a dare from Pete Peterson, after the shrink cleared me for the flight operations that I had already flown, thanks to the Sauffley doc's faux pas, I stopped at the shrink's doorsill, then hopped over it with both feet together like a bunny rabbit as I went out into the hallway.

Waiting on a bench outside like I knew he would be, Pete Peterson got a big laugh out of his dare because he already knew that I could resist almost anything but temptation. However, I did not have the time to stop and chew the fat with Pete because I had to get the heck out of that building before that scruffy ol' shrink could call me back and bang my ears for another session.

43. NAVCAD "PUPPY DOG" MALOOF

"Puppy Dawg" Maloof was a harmless little guy with soft doe-like eyes and a shy but always-ready crooked little smile. One day he confided to me that he had become a NavCad just to learn to fly his prosperous daddy's twin-engine Beechcraft while also getting out of other duties in the Navy. Even the rich kids were draft bait back then, and the Navy was the least of four bad choices for him.

However, he had somehow gotten ahead of his own secret schedule to become a competent multi-engine pilot, and then drop out of the program before being commissioned (for life: i.e., up to something like age 62) before he had logged the four years of his in-service requirement—including his time as an enlisted man—needed to be immediately discharged upon request. Puppy Dog did not want any part of that life-long commitment. He had more enjoyable things to do, but I hoped that he might change his mind.

Maloof was absolutely amazing. He would be standing in the middle of the cadet hanger, his name would be called for a flight that he did not want to fly, and he would disappear into thin air. Nobody could find him. I know, I tried several times with no luck. Finally, my CAC buddy, the Safety Officer, put a straight-back wooden chair in his own office's tiny closet where Maloof had to sit during any day when he had not yet logged a flight. The large, professionally hand-printed sign over the door read: "Maloof's Ready Room." Even then, Cadet Maloof managed to take twice as long to get through that segment of the syllabus as anyone else.

44. NAVCAD "BARF BAG" MARKHAM

Each NavCad carried a tightly folded, expandable paper bag in a thigh or shin pocket of his flight suit in case he would become airsick and toss his cookies while flying. I had the same type of barf bag mildewing in my right shin zipper pocket just below my right knee throughout my entire tour in the Pensacola Training Command. I never used it. I never needed it.

On the other hand, Cadet "Barf Bag" Markham was issued a fresh new barf bag almost every day that he flew. Except for straight and level flight (like cross-country navigation training for example.) with comparably gentle turns, Cadet Markham was likely to suddenly, without warning, spew his meager coffee and toast breakfast all over the airplane cockpit if he did not get his barf bag out of his pocket and deployed in time.

That was bad news for the flight line maintenance personnel, and worse news for the next guy who would get stuck with a closed canopy in an aircraft that Cadet Markham had just flown and upchucked. (News Flash: the cockpits of 14-year old training aircraft smell pretty bad from leaking fluids, sweat and even urine backed up from the urine relief tube. However, after Cadet Markham had done his predictable act, an enclosed cockpit could smell worse than a herd of constipated camels. That was bloody awful. I always checked to avoid any aircraft recently flown by Cadet Markham.

Ol' Barf Bag really did have a very sensitive stomach, but he did not want to go back to being an enlisted sailor until his total enlistment commitment was over. Therefore, at his request, I finally, as the Cadet Battalion Commander, took pity on the little guy and slipped him a gate pass so that he could eat lunch and supper off base if the chow hall menu did not agree with his super-sensitive digestive system.

If there ever was a cadet who was most certainly born to fly many motors, straight-and-level aircraft and only many motors aircraft, "Barf Bag" Markham was that guy. Straight and level will usually get you to your destination, but that is not a heck of a lot of fun along the way.

45. LOW AND SLOW

The PBY was an incredibly slow but reliable WWII amphibious patrol airplane that was still being used for air-sea rescue and reconnaissance. Most folks familiar with the old PBY jokingly claimed that it took off, cruised and landed at about 80 knots; not too fast. I discovered that one day when I was doing some solo low-altitude work and one of our guys crashed into a rough and remote forest near Spanish Fort, Alabama. I was the only guy who saw the wreckage, and I was the only guy who knew exactly where it was in the surrounding forest. Heck, I was the only other guy in the whole danged area late in that day, and there was no way that I could get down there and help the pilot who I could not see because of the dense forest.

So I made a low pass and wiggled my wings and raced my engine to let him know that I had seen the wreckage, headed for altitude and called a "Mayday" to the Air/Sea Rescue guys back at Pensacola. Not sure of the exact location, they told me to orbit the site to help direct them to the otherwise unknown crash site as quickly as possible.

So I climbed to something like 6,000 feet and setup an orbit above the crash site. Soon, I could clearly see the PBY coming my way at not much above tree-top level just west of Pensacola a fairly long distance away. As I came around the east side of my circle on each orbit, the PBY usually looked a little closer, but sometimes it just flat did not. Fast, it is not.

Although I was flying with a lean fuel mixture to conserve go-juice after flying a little more than three hours, including the post-crash orbit, I was beginning to get low on fuel so I passed the word to the NAS Sauffley control tower. Could they get another aircraft over the crash site to take my place? In a word, their answer was "no" because most of the cadets and instructors had come back to the barn already. They advised me to hold my position as ordered until the PBY arrived. Maybe 5 minutes later we went through the same rain dance; and then repeated it after that as I began to sweat my fuel situation.

I have mentioned that "Aye, aye Sir" in Navy/Marine lingo means "I hear you and I will obey." Like any good Marine, I carried out my orders to the best of my ability, so I stuck with it and was on the verge of a desperately low-fuel emergency by the time the PBY arrived. As soon as they spotted the crash site, they gave me permission to shove off. Since my fuel supply was getting seriously low and I did not want to run out of go juice at 500 feet altitude in the landing pattern, I requested a straight-in landing (rather than the usual carrier-type race-track pattern) because both wing tanks were drained and my main fuel tank was flirting with "empty" by then.

The answer: "No sale. Get in line." They weren't going to mess with the whole danged pristine landing pattern for one overly cautious NavCad airplane driver.

Fortunately, my approach and landing were normal, but as soon as I finished my landing roll out and turned onto the nearest taxi way to head for the barn, my engine stopped and suddenly I too could read the "Hamilton Hydromatic" decals on my propeller.

I remember that my initial thought was: "Aaa-haaa! I TOLD you clowns that I was low on fuel." Then I realized what could have happened if the darned fuel would have run out just a minute or so before when I was flying in the landing pattern at 500 feet or less over unforgiving terrain.

A round of drinks were on me at the Cadet Club that evening. I was still beating the odds, but that last one was way too close for comfort.

46. WHO SWIPED MY BASEBALL MITT?

My Rawlings T-70-RY Trapper mitt was the best and most expensive first-baseman's baseball glove of that era. Several years earlier, I had taken it in lieu of a $100 loan that I had made to Dwayne Wilson, an old neighborhood friend and sometimes team mate who later pitched for the Boston Red Sox.

One afternoon when I was playing an officers-versus-cadets baseball game at NAS Pensacola, I pulled a tendon in my leg while stretching for a low throw on a close play, and I had to be sidelined after the fifth or sixth inning. So I sat in the dugout and watched the remainder of the game while our coach, also a lefty, took my place at first base.

After the game was over, my expensive mitt was gone for good. I looked everywhere and talked to all who were on the field that day, but no luck. Incidentally, the only people at that game (players, umpires, coaches and spectators) were current or soon-to-be officers and gentlemen in the U.S. Navy or Marines. But one of those officers and gentlemen was not a gentleman.

Who'da ever thunk it? Initially, not me. But later…that's another story. Like Mr. Cowboy, the gnarled old night clerk at the Royal Hotel in El Dorado, Kansas often said: "We get too soon old and too late smart."

47 . FOREST FIRE BUGOUT

After watching the smoke of a raging forest fire in the distance for several days, Saturday morning about 100 NavCads were volunteered to reinforce the exhausted local fire fighters. As the Cadet Battalion Commander, I was responsible for the NavCads. That wasn't too popular with the local crackers who wanted to be in charge of every firefighter including all of our group of NavCads.

Right off the bat, we did okay as we saved several homes and outbuildings using nothing more than shovels, tree saws, and light equipment like that. However, we also lost a half dozen shacks that we could not get to in time because the local crackers did not want to add them to their list of priorities, especially during their lunch hour. Our NavCads could only do so much with what we had, but we gave it our best shot while the crackers enjoyed their scheduled lunch break.

Finally, after lunch we were spread out on a fire line several dozen yards into the forest from a rutted, dirt, one-lane country road when some idiot local jughead started a parallel backfire just on the other side of the road. Like the Irish often say, if something really bad can happen, it usually will. So naturally the wind shifted quite a bit and within no time at all, we had a wall of fire raging on both sides of us in the up-to 80-foot high trees and thick underbrush of northern Florida.

Our only chance to escape was to run like the dickens down that narrow, rutted dirt backwoods road for about half a mile to a huge green meadow. We had no choice, so we had to drop much of our heaviest fire-fighting gear and run like scalded apes while the fire closed in fore and aft, roaring and nipping at our backsides. It was truly "Lead, follow, or get the hell out of the way." Since these were my guys, I counted off my entire crew as they ran by me so I was the last one out. That gave me a real close-up view of not only the raging forest fire, but of all of our equipment being burned to cinders.

The next day, the winds died down to gentle breezes, and the great state of Florida finally brought in half a dozen bulldozers that made fire lines way too wide for the fires to jump. If those bulldozers had arrived a day earlier, we wouldn't have needed to wash all of that smoke out of our hair and dungarees Saturday night and the local crackers would still have a few more deep-woods shacks to fornicate in.

To this day, when I sit in a dark room and see a close-up of a raging forest fire on a wide-screen TV, I still get the heebie jeebies. Like they often said in various advanced Latin classes: "Nullum beneficium est impuntum" which I'm told translates to: "no good deed goes unpunished."

48. OLD SOCKS AND SEA BAGS

My good buddy, Marine NavCad George Baummerman, was a very large, easy going guy who had worked on the docks of Hoboken, New Jersey where they shot the movie "*On The Water Front*." He was about an inch taller than me, barrel chested, with heavily muscled arms and legs, and probably outweighed me by 25 to 30 pounds (figure 13). A semi-gentle giant, George had a terribly thick New Jersey accent and was usually a big ol' teddy bear looking for a good time. Aroused, he was something else.

The first time I saw George, some rascal had signed me up to box the heavyweight finale match in the ground-school interclass "smoker" the next week. When I checked in at hangar where the smoker would be held, I saw this large, muscular monster of a man climbing up and down a heavy rope to the hangar rafters by using only his hands (and no feet; no kidding!). I asked the officer in charge who that big guy was, and he told me that was George Bommerman, the heavyweight gorilla that I was scheduled to box in the next week's smoker. I tell you true, that shook my tree. Heck, I was not sure that I could climb that darned rope even using both my hands and my feet.

1954 MAKING A MARINE PILOT WARRIOR

Figure 13. George Bommerman (on the left),
One of the Good Guys and Dave Ferman (on the right)

The night of the boxing matches, George and I were sitting in the audience getting acquainted and watching the first of many boxing matches when we noticed that all of the cadets and officers in the audience were drinking icy cold, free keg beer and having a grand old time. Both of us agreed that was just flat unfair. However, since George and I were scheduled to box the last match, at which time they would shut off the free, ice cold beer spigot and all cadets would then return to our barracks, so although we were providing the entertainment, we could not wet our whistles with free, ice-cold Budweiser like everyone else in the building.

So George and I decided that we too should be able to drink free icy cold Budweiser beer as long as both of us would be drinking the exact same amount so that neither of us would have an alcoholic advantage.

For the next dozen or so matches, George and I sat side by side enjoying the free beer and watching the three-round, two-minutes per round boxing matches.

Long story short, once again my left-handed boxing style—moving constantly to my right so that right-handed George had to throw his best right-handed punch over his left (jabbing) hand—was to his disadvantage. That way, I was able to pop inside, throw a couple of good punches and then pop outside before George could counterpunch.

After the second of three rounds, George Bailey, who was acting as my manager in my corner, took a peek at the three judges' score cards and assured me that I had a commanding lead, so I should just take it easy during the third and last round. Boy, was that bad advice because when I took it easy and slowed down the pace, Baummerman caught up with me and landed a big roundhouse right hand right on my snotlocker, and I darned near hit the deck. Luckily, I tied him up with a clinch while I tried to remember what the heck I was supposed to be doing in that boxing ring.

Anyway, I stayed upright and finished the round which rightfully went to George. So I won two rounds, George won one, and we were good buddies ever after. In fact, we never had another beach party on the beautiful white sands of Pensacola Beach without George Baummerman front and center.

Then one evening after an exhausting day of flying six-plane formations with tight ten-foot step-downs (that can ruin your day in so many ways, even with just one finger on the joy stick),

George and I eased over to the "O" Club after supper to celebrate a commendation that I had just received from the C.O. at Sauffley Field (figure 14). We were just checking our hats with Dasie the hatcheck girl, when four brand-new shave-tail Marine 2nd lieutenants—they had just graduated from Quantico and still had the quartermaster's creases in their dress uniforms—lined up behind us. For some strange reason, all four of these guys took offense that George had picked up a potted palm nearby and was presenting it to Daisy as a tribute to her rare beauty (and her unmentioned but famously round heels).

We had problems right off the bat when all four of these guys began mimicking and making fun of George's New Jersey accent. Of course, George and I tried to laugh it off and keep everything low key, especially since we were in the "O" Club, which was a semi-hallowed place for most but not all officers and definitely all cadets. Somehow, these new shave-tails were looking for a bit of fun at our expense, and they just would not go away even though we stepped back and let them go first in line. Finally, we had to explain to these young 2nd lieutenants that George and I had more time in Marine Corps chow lines than they had in the Marine Corps between the four of them, and that we had worn out more sea bags than they had worn out socks.

Figure 14. This Commendation Was Not Misplaced in the Shuffle

Well, this led to that, and that led to the other, and the other led to their group of four challenging George and me to step outside the front door with them so that they could show us some of their newly ordained command presence.

Since George and I were thinking along the same lines, I gladly held the front door open as the four new 2nd lieutenants followed George outside. That was my big mistake because when I got out there right behind the last guy, three of the four newly commissioned young shave tails were already laying on the grass repenting their folly, and only the fourth newly commissioned 2nd lieutenant was still standing. However, he was closer to me than to George so I tossed him into a large ornamental bush and he didn't come out until after George and I returned to the "O" Club to continue our conversation with, and presentation to the lovely Daisy.

They say that USMC 2nd lieutenants wear a single goldish bar on their collars so that we can tell them from the real officers. From what I have seen, I would say that is a fairly accurate assessment.

49. I GO MONO

As a Marine grunt, DI and MP, and then as a NavCad often wearing Marine green uniforms, I had fooled myself to literally believe that as far as work was concerned, I was darned near superman without the cape. That is, if I set my mind to do something, I believed that I could get it done no matter what the difficulties or obstacles might be. If I could not go around an obstacle, I would go right over it, although my Grampa Volz in Iowa had told me that life is simpler when you plough around the stumps. If I could not do something in a 12-hour day, then by golly I would work harder and do it in a 14-hour day. If that wasn't enough, I would suck it up and do whatever needed in a 16- to 18-hour day.

Being a Marine Drill Instructor just re-enforced my overly ambitious self-image as a "can do" leader. Silly me. Real life does not always work that way.

So when I got to NAS Sauffley, I thought nothing of going to really challenging classes all morning that were graded on a curve (aerodynamics, celestial and DR navigation, radial engines, principles of flight, etc.) so that somebody had to fail each test; flying acrobatics, multi-plane formations, aircraft carrier-type landings, night flying, cross-country missions and aerial dog fighting with Lt. Paul Stretch after lunch; then hopping on a bus to Pensacola Mainside six days each week to play both offensive and defensive end as well as punter, point-after-touchdown kicker and even occasionally successfully field-goal attempter in college-level football games for the Pensacola Goshawks; all to make the Admiral happy.

The Admiral really loved "his football team" so several other NavCads and I had been transferred from NAS Whiting out in the boondocks 20 miles to the east of downtown Pensacola to much more accessible NAS Sauffley only 15 minutes from the football field at Mainside so that I could play on his football team, study football playbooks and ground school text books after supper, watch our game movies on Monday evenings and chalk talks on Wednesday evenings while entertaining visiting VIPs at the Pensacola Officers' Club, flying at least once each flyable day, as well as log my fair share of time at the beautiful and exciting Pensacola white sands beach and the far handier NavCad slop chutes with my guys.

Because of my duties as the Cadet Battalion Commander, I was the only cadet at Pensacola who had open-gate liberty any time of any day or night. Like they say: "Use it or lose it." I used it. For crying out loud, I wore it out.

Needless to say, I was dragging my donkey—physically and mentally bent all out of shape—but I would not/could not back off even if I wanted to. I knew that I needed to slow down, but there was no wiggle room worth mentioning left in my daily schedule. For example, we played Miami University in Miami, Florida, and Ft. Carson in Colorado on the road on two consecutive weekends. Those teams were good, really good, and really big, as were the Quantico Marines, the Great Lakes Navy base and the San Diego MCRD Marines.

My junior college team mate and good buddy, Forrest (Six) Scheifler, played defensive tackle for Ft. Carson in Colorado, so we knocked each other around pretty much during the whole darned game, mostly for our future, friendly bragging rights. I hardly remembered partying with

Six after the game, although when we got together eight years later when my wife and I lived in Denver, Six could not stop talking about what a great time he and I had together in Colorado Springs after that game. That was news to me; I really could not remember much of anything after the half-time break when I had to get a new bell to ring.

During those crowded, exhausting days, I flew five hops every week including check rides, and spent at least two evenings at the Officers' Club making Kodak Moments for various VIPs and friends of the Admiral, and as much time as I could spare while searching various honky tonk roadhouses for my One True Love. And of course, we had that monthly late-nighter with my Confederate Air Corps (CAC) buddies talking shop and laughing about each other's hilarious sea stories over a keg or two of beer and plates of blackened T-bone steaks a'plenty.

As the only NavCad to ever be inducted into the CAC, I felt honored to be accepted as an equal by Marine colonels and a Navy admiral or two in the local CAC at that time.

NOTE: everyone in the CAC held the honorary rank of Colonel, and everyone in the CAC was equal to every other CAC member regardless of Navy or Marine rank. That was quite a heady situation, but I buckled down and got comfortable with it fairly quickly. Like I said before, on several occasions I was the only pilot present who had not shot down a Japanese aircraft during WW II.

One of the better perks of the open gate pass was the notorious "Four O'clock Club located near beautiful Pensacola Bay. On a weekday liberty, almost all of the NavCads had to be back to their bases by midnight. Essentially, that meant every NavCad but me. Think about that for a minute. All evening I had serious competition in my never-ending search to find my "One True Love." A lot of NavCads had carte blanc to their wealthy parents checkbooks, but all I had was my measly NavCad pay check and not a penny more. On top of that, a lot of my competitors could dance. No kidding. Fred Astair I was not, nor did I really give a flip except for very slow, full-frontal, sensuous, shoe scooting dances.

No matter what happened before midnight, the commissioned Navy/Marine officers and I were about all the choices that the local gals had after midnight, and the Four O'clock Club did not close until, well, 0400. By that time, a goodly number of inevitable new-found couples had usually chosen up sides and disappeared into the balmy night air.

On the last evening that I played football for Pensacola, I needed a couple of bennies from Doc Feelgood, the team Corpsman, to get through the second half of the game. Then, somewhere around O-Dark 30, a bunch of my usual night owl friends decided to take our post-game party to the beautiful white sands of Pensacola Beach just for grins. Of course, nobody had a swimming suit handy, but darned near everybody had tightey whitey skivvies, so we improvised. In the dark before dawn, my Scotch plaid boxer shorts could easily pass for a swimming suit.

Then, when the waitresses from the Four O'clock Club arrived at the beach, one of the lovelier young ladies gave me the Big Eye, and I was kinda', sorta', maybe thinking that this fine young beauty might actually be my long-awaited One True Love at last.

Unfortunately, that fine young prospect and I joined a gaggle of cheerful drunks playing "King (and Queen) of the Mountain" on one of the lifeguard towers. In her black two-piece skivvies, my Four O' clock gal was winning overall until she slipped off the top rail of the tower, did a backward flip and landed flat on her back in the sand 10 feet below, which broke several ribs and bruised most of the rest of them.

Since I was the only semi-sober reveler on the beach that had any formal first aid training, I got the rose to take her and her car to the hospital where a gaggle of ER folks thanked me for my first aid skills, then told me to back off and get the heck out of their way so they could do their job; "dammit." Bottom line: with the bennies and branch water, I did not hit the sack until after high noon on Sunday.

The good times were wearing me down, but I was too darned dumb to slow down and smell the roses.

Then, several days later, after my usual morning inspection, while I was marching about 50 of my NavCads from the barracks to the flight line after my morning inspection, the lights suddenly went out and the pavement came up and kissed me hard; very hard indeed.

When I woke up the next day in sickbay with a split lip, bloodshot eyes and no energy at all, the middle-aged Navy doctor said that I had the worst case of mononucleosis that he had ever seen. Then he restricted me to bed rest, which translated to no exercise, no buxom serving wenches, no beach bunnies, no tequila shooters, and absolutely no stick time in the wild blue yonder. Like the song goes: "Turn out the lights, the party's over…" Aaaarrrrggggghhhh!

However, since I was still the NavCad Battalion Commander Dawg, each morning after intentionally missing breakfast (often my buddies would bring me coffee and a roll or something light) from the belly robbers, I would kinda', sorta' inspect the preflight formation, then have my second in command march them several blocks to the flight line while I returned to my bunk for the rest of the day. That went on and on and on for something like 9 or 10 long weeks. That was a lot of doggoned wasted days.

As soon as I was cleared for light duty, I went right back to flying. Thanks to my good buddies in the Confederate Air Corps, I even got some dual stick time in the T-28 and an AD-Queen Skyraider just for grins. The T-28 was very agile, had a far-more powerful engine than the SNJ, and was a real hoot to fly. That Skyraider, however, was essentially a big load that flew a lot like a combination oversized SNJ and a dump truck.

I had read everything I could find about both birds while I was semi-confined to my bed, and I could not wait to test myself in their cockpits. Thankfully, by the time I finally recovered, the football season was history, and the beach was too darned chilly for chasing beach bunnies let alone catching one.

My advice: be very very careful about what you ask for. God seems to have a sense of humor, so you might just get what you asked for, only tenfold.

50. STEALTH PRESCRIPTION GLASSES

One bright and cloudless afternoon, I lead a six-plane formation and the darned chase plane straight through another six-plane formation head-on at a closing speed of about 300 knots (a mile is 5,280 feet while a knot is 6,000 feet so do the math). Too late for evasive action, we passed straight through each others' formations like streaking yellow bullets in our peripheral vision. Nobody had the time to be scared or even flinch until it was all over and too late to reach for the urine relief tube.

Like many other cadets and even some instructors, my eyesight had been getting a little bit worse. Therefore, like so many others, I snuck over to a recommended eye doctor in Mobile, Alabama, and bought a pair of prescription glasses that corrected my vision to almost 20/20. However, that particular instructor/chase pilot had a sneaky habit of flying inverted close enough over the formation lead pilot to see whether or not he (i.e., me) was wearing glasses or just to take a peek into my cockpit for kicks.

Actually the chase pilot should have been on the lookout and seen the oncoming death and destruction hurtling head-on in our direction, but he was apparently too darned intent with playing games and flying inverted really close overhead while looking straight down at me from a distance of about 30 feet if that much. That was his big novelty trick, and he did it over and over again, and to hell with the idea of a second pair of eyes scanning the sky for added safety.

Remember, in a six-plane formation only the lead pilot is looking around. Everyone else is locked on those two aircraft check points to hold himself tightly in his exact location within the formation.

A couple of days later, I was in the middle of a check flight when Lt. Stretch told me to turn around and look at him in the rear cockpit. So I hunched my shoulders so that my flight jacket collar and helmet hid my hand, raised my goggles, removed my glasses, flipped my goggles back down and then turned around and looked back at him. He said "Nevermind" rather sarcastically. Maybe five minutes later, I was back to wearing my prescription glasses and again Lt. Stretch told me to turn around. So once again, I hunched my shoulders, raised my goggles, removed my glasses, flipped my goggles back down, and looked back at him. Lt. Stretch said: "Aw forget it." He never again mentioned glasses either in the air or before or after a flight.

In the Training Command, it was common knowledge that many of the commissioned Naval Aviators wore prescription sunglasses disguised as normal sunglasses. I could afford only one pair of glasses at my pay grade, so I bought the clear lenses that could be used for both day and night flying. Nobody ever questioned the guys who wore prescription sunglasses in front of God and everybody. Nobody wanted to break someone else's rice bowl, possibly because that could become a two-way street.

51. BIG BAD BUBBA THE THUNDER BOOMER

Flying in a six-plane formation that particular day (figure 15), I was in the number six slot, the last guy in the step-down formation; the tail-end Charlie who had joined the formation last. It was a beautiful day with towering cumuli nimbus thunder clouds boiling up to anvils topping out at about 50,000-foot altitudes if not higher. These are the big thunder boomers that breathed lightning and boiling updrafts a'plenty. I always loved to play around with small cumulus clouds that had big intervals between puffballs, but those that day were deadly monsters to be avoided. Only a fool or some weirdo with a death wish would get close to these widow makers in an SNJ.

Unfortunately, that fool was flying in the number-one (lead) position so, naturally, he was the only one able to look around because the rest of us were busy keeping the tail wheel of the next higher plane in the formation exactly aligned along each pilot's line of vision with the inside of the left inboard wing flap so as to give each pilot a rock solid position with the 10-foot step-down. Even with my vision locked on these lineup points, in my peripheral vision I could see that the lead pilot was flying awfully darned close to these beautiful but incredibly powerful updrafts. Where the heck was the instructor/chase pilot who should have been watching for such foolishness? I know that he was up there someplace, but I did not have a clue about what the heck he was doing. He sure as heck was not managing the store.

1954 MAKING A MARINE PILOT WARRIOR

Figure 15. Plane Formation For Ultimate Confidence

The next thing that I knew, the lead plane and the four guys tacked onto him had barely cleared the closest thunder boomer. However, as the last guy in the formation, I was dragged right into that darned cloud, and all I could see was the inside of my canopy as I was rolling end over end and side over side in six degrees of freedom like a continuous series of snap rolls until I had no spatial orientation since all of my instrument gimbals had just been tumbled because nobody cages them for a six-plane formation flight. I was trying to fight this monster, but was losing as I was getting banged around the cockpit until, suddenly, my little bird was tossed out of the blackness flying basackwards and at least 6,000 feet higher than my formation was flying.

That Principles of Flight class was absolutely correct. An airplane with dominant laminar flow aerodynamics is not controllable when sailing through the air basackwards. However, as it began a boomerang motion to my right, I gave it full right rudder and stick to continue that roll until I had sufficiently rotated far enough to begin a semi-controlled dive. As the airspeed picked up and the airfoils finally took over in my favor, I knew darned well that I had just beaten the odds one more time.

Thank you Jesus, Mary and hooooly St. Joseph.

Back at NAS Sauffley, the chase pilot/instructor disappeared before I could have a chat with him. He knew that he had messed up, and he did not want to talk about it with me while my hair was still on fire. However, the lead pilot, another of the jug-headed Navy ensigns who should have been a recreation officer on a tug boat, could not disappear so we had a spirited conversation about lead formation pilots flying too damn close to big thunder-boomer clouds so that the last guy or guys in the formation get all beaten up and spit out to fend for himself. Cornered, that squirrelly shave-tail's story was essentially that old vaudeville excuse: "I didn't do it, and I'll never do it again."

52. YA'LL HAIL THE SECRETARY OF THE NAVY

The by-gosh Secretary of the whole danged U.S. Navy (and thus the Marine Corps) visited Advanced Flight Training at NAS Sauffley Field late in November. Since I was the Cadet Battalion Commander and had a separate suite of rooms, for some darned reason The Great One and our Commanding Officer inspected my suite of rooms while I was flying, and some blabber mouthed fudge head found an empty half pint whiskey bottle on the deck behind my chest of drawers.

Of course, I had no idea where it could have come from. But nevertheless, the Base Executive Officer (X.O.) summoned me to his office to explain my faux pas that afternoon as soon as I landed.

When in deep doo doo, it is always a good idea to change the subject if at all possible. Like a wise man once said: "If you can't be sincere, fake it."

So I gave it my best shot by requesting permission to fly with the NavCad Choir to Denver, Colorado, that weekend to visit my mom and sort out her special plans before Christmas in Wichita. In the course of that rather tense discussion, the X.O. agreed to the trip and apparently blew off my faux pas in the confusion of the moment. That was my more complete version of the old "I didn't do it, nobody saw me do it, and I will never do it again, Sir" excuse. Surprisingly, it worked slicker than hydralube on a brass door knob.

During the flight to Denver in a Navy four-motor R4D (civilian DC-6) transport, somebody must have cut some corners on the in-flight sack lunches because right after we hit some fairly rough weather over Texas, a couple of the cadets tossed their cookies into their sack lunches. Then a few more were sickened by the smell and bouncing around, so they barfed all over the place as well until exponentially every single pilot and potential pilot aboard that large airplane, except yours truly and the flight crew, were upchucking all over the place with gut wrenching abandon. It was like the "1812 Overture" with stomach empting barfs instead of resounding cannon shots.

When we arrived in Denver, all of those choir guys were a mess. Then, when we looked out the side windows, we saw the Mayor of Denver, other VIP dignitaries and a gaggle of still and motion picture photographers assembled to greet the apparently famous NavCad Choir. Unfortunately, no one in the choir was in any condition to meet and greet with Hizz Honor the Mayor, a gaggle of other local VIPs, or anyone else. Panicked, the darn choir mutually begged me to represent them while they washed their faces and changed their uniforms. To a man, they all looked so pitiful that I could not refuse their whining petitions.

So I walked down the portable airport stairs solo, met the mayor and other assembled dignitaries, and posed for some grip-and-grin photos for the local newspapers while stalling for time. In fact, the ruse was going along fairly well until somebody asked me several esoteric questions about our choir and that evening's performance. That's when I had to admit that I was only the Cadet Battalion Commander and had nothing to do with the NavCad Choir performance.

Stop the music! Lower the cameras. Goodbye Dave or whatever your name is." They wanted to talk to the Choir Master, so I beckoned him to get out there mui pronto. Then I excused myself, walked over to the taxi cab lineup, and left the choir to their own devices. Like my buddy George Bailey often said: "When in doubt, punt."

When I arrived at Grandpa George and Grandma Amy's house on the south edge of downtown Denver just one block east of Broadway, I was flabbergasted to find that my dear old Mom was actually there. Holy cow! I had not fibbed to the X.O. after all, even though I was pretty darned sure that I had. And wouldn't you know that Mom wanted to have a nice dinner at the Officers' Club that evening when I was supposed to be on a date with Cousin Amy's gorgeous roommate.

So what the heck, Mom and Cousin Amy and I went out to the air base for a fairly early supper, and got the best table in the room for our purposes.

Even Mom's friends did not know that my Mom did not know anything about mixed drinks. She did not have even a clue. Mom was an occasional beer and wine-drinking amateur from Iowa, but that night she wanted a mixed drink just like in the movies. When she asked about that, I told her that ladies usually drink screwdrivers because they taste really good, and have a lot of orange juice in them. Mom loved orange juice. So when the waiter brought us our first adult beverages, on the sly I quietly told him to refill Mom's screwdriver drink automatically each time that she emptied it. I was hoping to salvage that hot date if at all possible.

All went very well, thank you very much. We had a great supper, and were able to take my Mom home snockered to her mama, Grandma Amy by 9 p.m., just in time for Cousin Amy and me to keep our pre-planned double date with Amy's blond and very pretty nursing school friend, and some guy for whom Amy had the big eye at that time.

Afterwards however, I've got to admit that I was a wee bit ashamed of the ruse that we pulled on Mom. However, in retrospect, I think it was probably worth it. Mom really had a good time that night, and she talked about it a lot when she got back to her friends in Wichita. Like they say back in downtown Kansas where I come from: "timing has a lot to do with the outcome of a rain dance."

53. MERRY CHRISTMAS 1954

The Ferman family had a great Christmas in 1954. It couldn't have been better. My older brother, Dick, came home from the Air Force Drum and Bugle Corps in Washington, DC; my younger brother, Mike, came home from Aerial Photo Interpretation School in the Army; I came home from Pensacola; and Marilyn was still at St. Mary's Cathedral High School in Wichita. Mom wanted us to wear our uniforms to Midnight Mass, but somehow we didn't. I don't remember the details, but we didn't. Then Jack McDonald showed up in his Air Force cadet uniform, so we heard about that from Mom right in the middle of the Mass. Mom didn't whisper softly that day.

Jack and I talked for a few minutes after Mass on the church steps, and I asked how many Air Force cadet pilots had been killed in training that year. He looked at me like I was from outer space and said: "Fatalities. We don't have no damned fatalities." Of course, the Air Force cadets were flying brand new Beechcraft T-34 trainers and had nothing to do with aircraft carrier landings or formation flying before being commissioned and receiving their wings. And despite the civvies at Mass, nothing could mess up that great Christmas, and our family reunion from the far-flung corners of the United States.

While at home, I was the first NavCad to fly the Beechcraft T-34 Mentor aircraft. Back at Pensacola, my buddies and some flight instructors had asked me to go out to my former employer, Beech Aircraft Company, and learn as much as I could about this new airplane that the Navy would eventually add to its cadet training stable. I was glad to do it.

The USAF acceptance pilot at Beech, Captain Neil Kemper (figure 16), insisted that I fly the T-34 for an afternoon of acrobatics and touch-and-go landings. It was such a delight to be flying a brand new airplane for a change. The T-34 was a really easy aircraft to fly from the moment I strapped it on.

During our first climb-out, Captain Kemper put the T-34 into a stall and then an intentional spin at about 1,000 feet of altitude, and recovered with plenty of space to spare. I was absolutely astounded and could hardly believe it. With our old junker SNJs, we had been restricted from full stalls and then a spin below 6,000 feet because we were told to bail out if still spinning out of control below 5,000 feet. Then the good Captain let me do every acrobatic maneuver that I had ever flown, including a climbing victory roll as an encore.

For about a nanosecond, I was tempted to try an outside loop before good sense trumped my curiosity. Everything else was open season, and I made the most of it. We beat the heck out of a whole bunch of clouds, and I enjoyed every minute of it.

Figure 16. Pre-flight Checkout with T-34 Aircraft

Quite a few people were assembling on the runway along with Mama Beech as I shot several picture-perfect touch-and-go landings without ruining the nose wheel of the tricycle landing gear with my full-stall, Navy aircraft-carrier landings, but the transition was no problem at all; it was seamless.

Afterwards, the Wichita Beacon, the Wichita Eagle and Beechcraft corporate photographers and reporters made it a bunch of Kodak Moments that were splashed all over both newspapers and various Beech Publications.(figure17).

All of that would be difficult to explain to my C.O. back in Pensacola because that flight was not authorized and I was, after all, government property. Thank goodness that the Navy and Marines received quite a bit of really good publicity from that dog-and-pony show. If not, my C.O. at NAS Sauffley could have kicked my donkey over the goal posts just as he should have when I mucked up that unexpected, unscheduled SecNav's visit due to lousy personal housekeeping just one month before that fine day. Actually, when I called my C.O. to tell him what I had done, the first thing that he said was "How does it fly?"

Figure 17. Post-Flight Marketing Photograph

54. NIGHT FLYING NIGHTMARES

Back at Pensacola, I continually lost my night-flight formations again and again because in the dark my minor color blindness made all of the airplanes' running lights look white to me. That was another unexpected surprise that made it difficult to differentiate between airplanes and stars when flying below the formations with which I was trying to join up, or between airplanes and ground lights when flying above the designated assembly areas and altitudes. Likewise, it could have been suicidal to fly at the assigned altitude while looking for my formations because we could possibly have collided.

As my Saxon ancestors had prayed during the Dark Ages: "From Goblins and Ghosties, and dark lurking Beasties, and things that go BOOMP in the night; Dear Lord deliver us."

After those fanny puckering occasions, I always took off at night as the second element in an unauthorized dual formation with "my wingman," Cadet Bob Gilbertson; he on the left side of the runway and me on the right side. I stayed in close formation with him by focusing on his fiery engine exhaust at the right side of his cowling. Nothing else in the air looked like that, and I had no trouble identifying the exhaust signature, especially whenever I saw it from pretty much up close and very personal in the dark night sky.

I remember that Cadet Gilbertson was really spooked the first time that he looked back and suddenly realized that I was flying a loose formation on him at about a 20-foot step down in the dark. When he squawked over the assigned channel, I told him to hush-up, keep flying, and go find the rest of the darned formation. Not being any bit red/green color bothered, ol' Bob usually got us into the right formation fairly quickly.

To paraphrase an old adage, there is more than one way to skin a bat.

55. "WHAT A HELLOVA' WAY TO DIE."

During a simulated high-altitude emergency test, as I descended from about 8,000 to 1,500 feet, I got crosswise with the incoming landing pattern at NAS Cecil Field. Impulsively, the checkout pilot jerked the control stick away from me, and threw us into a tight left turn much too abruptly. That quickly turned into a steep-turn stall to the left that went over the top to an inverted stall just below something like 1,500 feet of altitude. Remember, mandatory bailout was at 5,000 feet.

As he tried to recover too quickly, that turned into a progressive stall at about 1,200 feet as he pulled back too hard on the stick too soon. To get us out of that usually fatal situation, he put us in a terminal dive to regain aerodynamic control. At that ridiculously low altitude, it was the only chance we had. Too late to bail out, the check pilot thought he was fighting both the aerodynamic pressures and me, so I put both of my hands on top of my helmet so he could see from the back seat that the intense control stick pressures were not coming from this doomed NavCad pilot.

In a terminal dive somewhere between 600 to 700 feet of altitude, I was looking straight down through my propeller at the earth directly in front of me, and I found myself saying "What a hellova' way to die. What a hellova' way to die!" over and over again when I should have been rapidly atoning for my many sins, promising my eternal commitment to be good, and pleading for divine mercy.

Somehow, the check pilot pulled out below the tallest tree tops (I am not kidding) which were approximately 80 feet high and more than 250 knots of air speed. Looking back, I believe that was pretty near that airplane's red-line airspeed. I just knew that something critical could be popped off that old junker at any second, and then we would have no chance at all since we were that close to the ground.

Back at the base, as we were walking back to the hangar, the check pilot admitted that he had screwed up a metric potful. I readily agreed, but the rules said that I could not reverse the order and give him a down for that flight.

Right after my debriefing, I bumped into the Safety Officer, my fellow Confederate Air Corps buddy, and told him that if I would never fly with that fudge-headed check pilot again, it would be too soon. For whatever reason, I never did.

Looking back, that check pilot might well have said about the same thing to the Safety Officer about me. However, I knew that low-level emergencies like that would get a whole heck of a lot more survivable after the Navy finally loosened their purse strings and popped for a gaggle of Beechcraft T-34 Mentors. As far as I was concerned, eee-mediately would not be too soon.

56. GARBAGE MOUTHED WAVE

As I believe I mentioned before, the most garbage-mouthed person I ever met was a career Navy Wave who had worked as a mechanic with one of my sailor-turned-NavCad friends. She was far worse than that female DI at MCRD, if that was possible. Not a bad looker as seen in the evening's inadequate light while sitting on the NAS Wave barracks front stoop, this gal lowered the bar to about six sexual derivative words out of any ten words spoken, and then most of the remaining words were scatological.

I was amazed that she could string together an actual sentence so readily with all of those vile nouns, verbs, adverbs and adjectives interjected, but she did it again and again with rapid-fire enthusiasm and a big dollop of jolly self-entertainment.

I guarantee you that those 30 to 40 minutes while sitting on the front stoop of the base Wave barracks eating watermelon and hearing about some of her more sleezy sexual misadventures, as well as those of her Wave friends, were some of the longest minutes of my life. Actually, I think that she scared the dickens out of me. I was afraid that I would catch something bad-nasty just by being in proximity to her, so I definitely was not interested in dating her no matter how much free watermelon that she gave me. I had my standards. I could not be bought, at least not with just one darned, tepid watermelon.

57. SKY KING

Back in about 1939 when I was a scrawny little whippersnapper, I usually hurried home from first grade to listen to the Sky King radio program at 5:15 p.m. The fact that Sky King was sandwiched between the Lone Ranger and Tonto program at 5 p.m, and Terry and the Pirates at 5:30 p.m. made no nevermind. Sky King could hold his own in the imaginations of all of the other little guys in the neighborhood. I could not wait to hear "C.X.4 to control tower. C.X.4 to control tower. Standing by," followed by the deep doppler-like roar of a powerful

1954 MAKING A MARINE PILOT WARRIOR

twin-engine airplane buzzing the microphone much too close overhead. That was the stuff of childhood hero worship.

Nobody could beat Sky King when he was at the controls of his incredibly invincible airplane. In our big sand pile in our back yard, and at recess at school when the little girls were giggling about patent leather dress-up shoes and lace ruffles galore, we little guys often swapped our impressions of the previous evening's program, and speculated about how Sky King would survive the latest cliff hanger which closed every program. After all, who could possibly defeat Sky King when he was at the controls of his sleek, powerful airplane that always arrived just in time to save the fair lady and toss the dastardly villain into the Crossbar Hotel?

While practicing solo advanced aerobatics just east of Mobile Bay, all of that flashed through my mind one severe-clear afternoon between 5,000 and 10,000 feet altitude over the Florida panhandle and the gulf coast. There, about 1,500 to 2,000 feet below me, I saw a single vulture lazily gliding along in the other direction on the afternoon thermal updrafts. Since I can usually resist just about anything except temptation, I peeled off and setup a diving mock gunnery run just for the pure fun of it.

Diving on that big bird from behind at something in excess of 200 knots (remember that a knot is 6,000 feet and a mile is 5,280 feet), I had all of the advantages for an easy "kill" if I would have machine guns in my wings. That is, I thought that I had the advantages until I almost had him bore-sighted when he reversed his direction almost on a dime so that he quickly passed under me without interrupting his effortless gliding attitude.

Since the SNJ did not have an outside loop in its repertoire, I extended my dive into a half loop with an Immelmann roll on the top so that the bird and I were both flying essentially in the same relative positions as before, except that then we were both headed east instead of west, and I was at about 8,500 feet altitude while the nimble vulture was maybe 1,200 feet below me, and still gliding casually along as if I was not worth his attention.

Since we were both flying in the same direction with the vulture out in front, this time I dumped my nose into a straight ahead dive, but I had a shallower angle at a reduced air speed—maybe 180 knots—while I maneuvered again for a better practice shot. However, that darned vulture reversed course again and descended fairly rapidly so that I lost him as I inverted to search for him, then split "S'ed" into an inverted dive to try to jump him again.

Suddenly he gained maybe 1,500 feet just as effortlessly as he had earlier lost about the same amount of altitude. Instinctively, I extended that split "S" into a loop, picked up maybe 900 to 1,000 feet of altitude, then rolled into another Immelmann turn, blacked out from the sudden negative G forces, and recovered just in time to find him above me casually headed in his original direction of flight. About that time, I finally recognized that this vulture was nature's equivalent of Sky King, my hero from my childhood.

For the next 15 minutes or so, ol' Sky King pulled me into target fixation a number of times when he lured me into an ever increasing, steeper dive until I suddenly found myself overextended in a terminal dive down through the 5,000 foot altitude imaginary "hard pan" that represents the ground level when training for air-to-air dog fighting.

If that wasn't enough, no matter what I did to gain the upper hand—including a double snap roll to slow down and showoff a little myself, several barrel rolls to keep him acquired, an unintended hammerhead stall when he popped up like a homesick angel headed for the heavenly barn with me right behind him, and even a faulty, underpowered victory roll that turned into a horizontal slow roll—ol' Sky King eluded my every pass, and then led me into another frustrating miss.

Just when I finally became fully aware that both wing fuel tanks were empty, and my main fuel tank was getting there quicker than I thought, that big bird and I were flying parallel at the same altitude with maybe 40 yards or less of lateral separation when I swear he casually looked over at me, smirked, then peeled off and headed west toward Mobile Bay where Jimmy Buffett's kin probably still worked that moonshine still out in the deep, woodsy boondocks.

Adios Sky King, and thanks for the flying lesson. You made my day.

58. MARDI GRAS IN NEW ORLEANS

A bunch of us Marine NavCads decided to drive down to New Orleans for the 1955 Mardi Gras on 72-hour passes. The five of us—George Bailey, George Baummerman, Joe D. (Jody) Bolling, Dick "Firecracker" Welch and I—were all pretty big guys, which made it even worse when we could not find a room in New Orleans on our first night in town. So we all had to sleep in Bailey's Oldsmobile coup. Rest assured, you have to be really good friends to make that work.

The next morning, we knew that we were in deep doo doo, so we called Cpl. Ed Krieger's family (who owned Krieger Tire Company on Canal Street) and asked if he was home, although we all knew for darned sure that he was still at the Naval Ammunition Depot in Nevada.

Overflowing with southern hospitable, Mrs. Krieger asked where we were staying. When I told her we were sleeping in Bailey's car, she insisted that we come over to their large house in the antebellum American District where they had plenty of rooms for all five of us. Don't you just love it when a cockamamie plan actually blunders together?

We could not have had better accommodations or more fun at Mardi Gras. The crowds were huge and out to have good, raucous fun. The bars in the French Quarter were in their prime as popskull flowed like water down the Mississippi River and in just about the same quantities. When we were hungry, we would stop by the Krieger kitchen where a huge steel caldron of red beans, rice and crawdads sat warming on their stove 24 hours every day.

That first night when we returned to the Krieger home a little after midnight, grandma Krieger met us in her kitchen and said: "This is a carnival night. You boys get back out there right now and celebrate some more." We were in hog heaven, so we bellied up to the trough, rinsed our bowls, and let the good times roll.

At Pat O'Brien's Bar that night, the crowd had been so densely packed that when some drunk did not want his girlfriend to get up on the stage and shimmy to "I Wish I Could Shimmy Like My Sister Kate" played over and over again by an out-dang-standing Preservation Hall-like band, the crowd picked up the soused boyfriend and joyfully passed him overhead and out the side door. I do not know if he and his sweetie ever got back together that night. She loved the stage and all of the attention that she was getting, and he could not push his way back to the stage due to the tightly pack crowd that was going crazy over his girlfriend's shimmy shaking antics.

That well soused crowd loved each and every exhibitionist southern belle who followed, and always yelled for more. They certainly had their way as the tipsy lunatics ruled the asylum.

Later that night, George Baummerman and I were jammed in a crowd just a few feet inside The Court Of Three Sisters front door while listening to a very good jazz band when Robert Mitchum, the Hollywood actor, apparently bumped or jostled George to get by him and into the club. As big as he was, George was always very polite. He was a real gentleman, but for some reason, Mitchum was getting madder and madder while George apologized several times for whatever Mitchum was bent about. Finally, Mitchum got nose-to-nose with George and bellowed: "Do you know who I am? I'm Robert Mitchum, and I'm going to kick your ass."

As Mitchum made some kind of an aggressive first move that I did not see, George popped Mitchum just once on his nose, and Mitchum went down like a sack of potatoes and, to continue the metaphor, he was out like Lottie's left eye. As we stepped over the unconscious movie star tough guy to leave before the fit hit the shan, George looked down at Mitchum and said apologetically: "I told you that I was sorry." George was always a gentleman

The Krieger daughter who was about 18 to 20 years old and walked with the most hip-swinging, come-and-dance-with-me swagger that seemed to be in tune with Jimmy Forrest's gut-bucket rendition of *Night Train*. Right off the bat, she and Firecracker Welch both seemed to have the mutual big eye for each other, so we naturally figured that her strut and her long, slow, sideways glances were all for Dick Welch's benefit. However, the next morning when we went to Mass with the Kriegers, she walked exactly the same way when she went up to the altar for Holy Communion. For heaven's sake, she wasn't putting us on: that was just the way that young lady naturally walked.

Then, after Mass and some more red beans and rice, we threw ourselves back into the debauchery that was the French Quarter just three days before Ash Wednesday. I kid you not, we had one heck of a good time.

We really hated to leave New Orleans behind while there was still any excuse to get loud and crazy. However, duty called, and by driving all night and taking turns behind the steering wheel, we got back to Pensacola with only one hour to spare on our 72-hour passes. It was, indeed, a full life and we loved it a lot. Who could ask for anything more? Not me.

Thank y'all Krieger family, we'll never forget you..

59. ADMIRAL CADET

While I was the Cadet Battalion Commander at NAS Sauffley, every noncommissioned student pilot prepping to move to Cecil Field for flight operations on the aircraft carrier USS Monterey reported to me. Then there were the commissioned cadets who competed with us in classes that were graded on a curve and flew with us noncommissioned NavCads as equals while we were in the air. To them, I held the temporary rank equivalent of major and had that much influence during our normal operations. However, off the base, they were still the commissioned officers and we were not.

Then there was a very young, athletic looking one star Navy admiral who was going through the flight-training syllabus on an incredibly abbreviated schedule. Of course, that admiral had his own team of instructors who were—oh gee—under the command of that same admiral. That had to be awkward and could have been quite dangerous, especially for the admiral because he could not have been trained as well as we who went through the normal syllabus and flew many, many more hours than he could have during the incredibly short time that admiral was at Sauffley.

With initial flight training (18 flight hours to the first solo flight in the best, newest SNJ-6s on the base, but even those late versions were pretty much gut shot), acrobatics, formation flying in two-plane then four-plane and then six-plane formations with 10-foot step downs, cross-country navigation, unusual attitudes under a canvas hood so the cadet can see only his instruments and nothing outside of the aircraft, air-to-air dog-fighting one-on-one with combat tested Naval Aviators, aircraft carrier landing simulations in racetrack landing patterns both day and night, as well as about ten weeks of ground school to prepare for, and support all of that stuff. That's a pretty tight syllabus for anyone.

However, that young-looking admiral apparently passed muster on all of those essentials because he graduated from Sauffley and progressed to actual carrier landings on the USS Monteray, all in just two weeks or maybe less. In my seldom humble opinion, that youngish admiral lusted for Navy Wings of Gold to pin on top his other decorations as a more-perfect pathway to bigger and better naval career horizons.

Since none of us NavCads were privy to his name (no kidding), we could not keep track of him because, without his entourage, he looked like an instructor and got lost in the crowds in the flight hangar. However, I did not see him and his entourage around the training hanger more than a couple of times on any of those few short days of training.

I just hope that high-ranking student pilot did not—like John John Kennedy—attempt to fly too much airplane with too little training, especially under any kind of adverse conditions. All of that training is intended to keep the student pilots alive, day or night and in all kinds of weather.

Would I fly with or beside that young admiral? Not only "no," but "HELL NO!"

FYI: That reminds me of my good friend Navy Commander Roy "Killer" Johnson who went through Navy flight training at the exact same time as George H. W. Bush during WW II. With 51 different aircraft listed in his flight log (including a Soviet MIG-15 fighter that he flew at NAS Moffett Field at the same time that I was stationed there as an MP), and the fact that Killer often flew CAP high-altitude, first-line defense for several carrier battle groups, showed that the Navy considered him a Top Gun fighter pilot. I was particularly impressed with his Navy citation for old-fashioned, face-to-face gun-fighting when he destroyed not one, but three armored, anti-aircraft protection-carrying trains in

North Korea within only a few weeks while flying a F4U Corsair prop job. That will get you an air medal award just about any old time.

Funny coincidence, back in about 1989 or so, I read G.H.W. Bush's story, and was amazed to see that he graduated and reported aboard his aircraft carrier in the Pacific Theatre exactly 10 months after he first reported for NavCad flight training. Remembering the quick-study admiral fly guy, I asked Killer Johnson how Bush did that when the normal flight school was 18 months. Killer told me that was just flat not possible even under wartime conditions.

Ooops. That explained a lot. I had to bring that book to work because Killer was so certain that I must have miss-stated those dates. They were just too unbelievable.

While he was at it, Killer reminded me that dive bombing with its negative high G pullouts is a young man's game. Usually unable to physically handle such high G's, older pilots normally do some other types of flying, particularly with multi-motor aircraft flying straight and level while brewing many cups of coffee to go with the ubiquitous doughnuts and Danishes. But when Ensign George H. W. Bush went into combat for the first time, he was given the relatively safe, high-altitude observer assignment that was always before assigned to a much older, more experienced pilot who would understand what he was seeing way down there at sea level, and could accurately report enemy battle damage and tactics back to Naval Intelligence.

As Killer assured me, an 18-year old shavetail ensign is not qualified to handle that job except, of course, when that shavetail is the son of an advisor to the President of the United States: Franklin D. Roosevelt.

Fortunately, when Ensign Bush was shot down anyway, there was a submarine on the spot that saved Ensign Bush's bacon. Funny thing though, for many years the former Ensign Bush told one and all that he was shot down by a Japanese fighter aircraft that day. Years later, just before that former young Naval Aviator ran for President of the United States, a Marine fighter pilot, who had also been in the same battle at about the same altitude that day, categorically denied that there were any Japanese aircraft in the air at that location on that day.

That's when the future President of the United States, George H. W. Bush, suddenly remembered that he was shot down by high altitude anti-aircraft fire, and his rear seat gunner was killed when he could not overcome the Gs of the falling, spinning aircraft and apparently rode the crippled aircraft all of the way down to splash in the ocean. There is more, but that's enough to get the picture.

Needless to say, many years later, I could not vote for G.H.W. Bush; not until little Michael "Duc-whatever his name showed up riding atop a huge tank with his ultra-wacky liberal revolving door policy about week-end passes for Murderers' Row. Then, I had far less trouble voting for G.H.W. Bush because there was no other viable choice.

60. STRESS IS A BOOGER BEAR

A couple of days later, I had pre-flight inspected my aircraft on the flight line, and was getting ready to go beat up some clouds on a solo acrobatic flight. As I stepped onto the foot step protruding from the outside of the fuselage on the left side of the aircraft, I looked down to make sure that my foot was in the right place before I put my weight on it. Something was not right. So I looked again, and just below my raised foot, I noticed that many of the rivets that connected the fuselage skin to the left wing root skin were popped off; apparently from excessive stress.

The last pilot that aircraft had, somehow put so much negative stress on that airplane that the aluminum "skin" had sheared about two dozen rivets in a row, and by regulation that damage should have been reported by the last pilot to fly it, and the aircraft should have been declared unsafe to fly and then grounded for overhaul.

To have suffered that much stress to the connective skins was a sure sign that the main wing spars inside the wing must have been badly overstressed—possibly by an extremely hard full-stall landing—and undoubtedly needed overhaul and/or replacement. Since I was not in a rush to die that day, I went back to the hangar and checked the squawks for damaged aircraft, but none were posted for that particular aircraft.

Obviously, somebody needed to grab the pilot who had flown that plane last and congratulate him for surviving that flight, then kick his butt for not reporting whatever the major incident that damaged that airplane so badly. It was criminal to leave an airplane in that condition for some unsuspecting pilot to fly. Because they flew a different airplane for every flight, again and again some of our commissioned Naval Aviators were not about to report anything that could affect their next efficiency evaluation and promotion.

Once again, flight line regulations were apparently intended for everybody except for the "good ol' boys" and the "ring knockers." Do I hear an "Aaa-men," Buddy Bubbas? I should.

61. I CRASHED, BURNED, AND DARN NEAR DROWNED

On the day that my SNJ Texan aircraft crashed, burned, and I darn near drowned in the brackish waters of that stale Florida swamp, everything was initially A-Ok and cooking on all burners. That was, indeed, another fine day for an hour or two of solo aerobatics hijinks in the severe-clear morning sunshine. In my seldom humble opinion, aerobatics in the wild, blue yonder are the most fun that a young cadet pilot can have with his clothes on. (Figure 18).

Unfortunately, when I added power to begin my takeoff roll, that previously damaged old bird hiccupped, sputtered, and then just sat there on the duty runway blocking traffic. My assigned SNJ suddenly did not have enough power to even begin the takeoff roll. So I eased off the manifold pressure and signaled the cadet pilot on the other side of the runway to go ahead and take off before me so that I could checkout that possibly significant hiccup. However, that blockhead just sat there looking at me like a village idiot while the lines of SNJs following each of us got longer.

Figure 18. A Good Day To Thrash a Few Clouds

Anxious to get the heck out of the way of the rapidly forming queue, for some darned reason I thought "Aw heck, let's go for broke," and pushed the manifold pressure to full take-off power again. Well darned if I didn't start rolling just as the other cadet woke up and decided to finally do the same thing, so that both of us were accelerating down the runway side by side, but with a fairly safe lateral space between us.

That was not as unusual as you might think because I had done that forbidden ploy intentionally on several night takeoffs in order to stick close to Bob, my usual wingman who had a lot better night vision than yours truly. So I figured that mildly iffy situation was no big deal; that is, it wasn't until my main landing gear wheels lifted off the runway and my SNJ lost the lateral friction between my rubber tires and the runway tarmac.

Immediately, my right wing snapped up from the horizontal and came very close to being fully vertical. Startled, I was sure that I was just about to drag my left wing-tip on the tarmac, cartwheel right there on the runway, and bow out in a big ugly ball of explosive fire and black greasy smoke. At the same time, I felt like a huge, open hand was underneath my airplane pushing me hard to the left toward the swamp and that other cadet's SNJ as well.

Instinctively, I slammed full right joy stick and kicked hard right rudder, but my plane continued flying to the left while I crossed directly over the other cadet with my left wingtip passing within inches of his open canopy. As I looked straight down at him from only a few inches more than the length of my SNJ's left wing above him, he seemed to go catatonic as he stared straight up at me as if I was the avenging angel of death. That poor guy had really big blue eyes. I could see them as plain as day.

Unable to recover, I grabbed my radio microphone and yelled "Mayday, Mayday, MAYDAY, I'm going down. I'M GOING DOWN!" The control tower operator calmly responded: "Ahh Roger. Where are you, Mayday?" I yelled back at him: "I'm right in front of you, DAMMIT!" Again, the tower calmly replied: "Ah yes, I can see you now."

Days later, at the post-accident analysis meeting, I recognized the tower operator—Roe Messner, who later married Tammy Faye Baker the televangelist—because he was our batboy when his older brother Bobby and I played for the championship T-Men Little League baseball team in Wichita, Kansas, way back in the summer of 1945 when I was 12 years old.

Like somebody important often said: "It is, indeed, a very small world."

With my SNJ still out of control and barely flying in that extremely dangerous attitude—especially since I was flying that close to the ground—I was sure that I would "buy the farm for Mom and Dad," and was just about to be null and void. With the manifold pressure still firewalled at full takeoff power, I had already passed over the edge of the wet-lands swamp that laid parallel to the far north end of the runway.

After pulling up my landing gear and the rest of my wing flaps, my wings rotated through straight and level, then further to the right for a change as I stayed fairly low to pick-up as much airspeed as possible. Just when I was sure that I was about to snap into a steep-turn stall and flip over inverted to crash into the brackish black water only a matter of feet below me, my SNJ somehow righted itself once again. At that faster airspeed, my wounded old airplane headed for altitude like a homesick angel.

As terror turned into relief, I knew that I was still in deep doo doo, but at least I had beaten the odds one more time. However, I wasn't out of the frying pan by a long shot.

The Flight Safety Officer—a Navy lieutenant commander who was a friend as well as one of the good ol' boys in our still somewhat clandestine Confederate Air Corps back when the CAC was composed of current and former Navy and Marine fighter pilots—he got on the horn and told me to take that sick old junker to altitude and give it a stall test. So I carefully flew up to about 9,000 feet altitude and then stalled my SNJ in the normal wings-level attitude.

Bad news: the darned thing stalled violently with a snap. That was not anywhere near normal. At more than 22 knots of air speed too soon, that was a complete surprise. Then, it did not recover from that spin in a turn and a half as advertised. In fact, it spun continuously, totally out of control until I was several thousand feet below the 5,000-foot mandatory bailout altitude before I could get it sorted out and somewhat under control when I picked up air speed by dumping my SNJ's nose even further downward.

Apparently perplexed, or maybe he was just stalling to buy some more time to launch the Air/Sea Rescue's PBY amphibious aircraft, the Safety Officer told me to fly back up to a 12,000-foot altitude and stall that sick old junker again. However, that time he wanted me to read him the decreasing airspeed numbers down to the exact onset of that unusually violent, snapping stall beginning with the wings level.

It was gut-check time because I had to maintain a faster air speed while gaining altitude or my SNJ could have snapped into a stall on the way back up to altitude. A chilling revelation, I realized that could have happened the first time when I had not understood the aerodynamic danger of the normal climbing speed in that condition. But like any good Marine, I followed orders and did what I was told to do, and had darn near essentially the same results.

The consensus quick-look analysis indicated that my SNJ was no longer capable of flying at about 22 knots above the normal stalling speed in a wings-level and otherwise clean configuration. Furthermore, it was not a good idea to execute a Navy/Marine full-stall carrier-type landing, or even approach the duty runway in the standard racetrack landing pattern where it could stall even sooner while in a turn; i.e., possibly at 30 knots or more above the normal stalling speed and too darned low to recover from that stall and subsequent spin.

Also, I was fairly sure that I would have to bail out after falling more than eight spinning turns or so. However, I really did not want to do that, especially since one of my guys had recently bailed out at below 5,000 feet and was killed when his parachute did not fully open. That was definitely on my mind at that time, so I stuck with that sick old SNJ a lot longer than I should have. Silly me.

The next thing that I knew, the Safety Officer told me for the record what we both already knew: that out-of-rig, old, pre-WW II hunk of worn-out junk had undoubtedly been grossly boogered on the previous flight, and was not only unsafe to fly, but it was really unsafe to land. He advised me that I should trim my plane for straight and level flight at cruising speed, aim it south over the gulf coast and bail out. By that time, a WW-II PBY amphibious Air/Sea Rescue plane was already in the air and would soon be waiting for me to splash.

However, since my flight was originally not meant to be an overwater flight, my Mae West flotation vest was still hanging in my equipment locker back at the hangar. So if you think the Safety Officer's plan was a comforting thought, you have another think coming to you.

That was also particularly bad news because at times of severe stress—like that flight most definitely was—I would apparently pump way too much adrenaline in my body, and my perception of time would go from real-time to slow-motion time like I described in far more detail in one of my earlier books: *Ghosts That I Have Known*. Therefore, if I jumped and the parachute once again became a streamer instead of fully deploying, that fall to eternity would possibly seem to go on and on for a heck of a long time before I would suddenly meet my Maker.

However, if I jumped over water, splashed in the bay and then got tangled in my parachute riser lines without my Mae West flotation vest, I would be damned if I did jump and damned if I didn't jump. Either way, my $10,000 military life insurance would probably "buy the farm" for Mom and Dad.

The Safety Officer and I talked a while about various crash list fundamentals, but I was still not enthusiastic about bailing out. Finally, I told him quite brashly—but as one Confederate Air Corps (CAC) Colonel to another CAC Colonel rather than as a noncommissioned NavCad to a Navy Lt. Commander—that I was in command of that aircraft, and I choose to attempt to land it while flying straight and level at a much faster airspeed than normal.

I really did not give a flip how my friend the Safety Officer would explain that whole rain dance to the Admiral's Safety Board, but I wanted to be there when it happened.

After about 30 minutes of messing around to get our arms wrapped around all of the potential contingencies, possibilities and survival procedures, the Safety Officer cleared every other aircraft out of the north/south landing pattern, and allowed a straight-in approach from about 15 miles north of the runway so that my wings could stay as level as possible while my airspeed would be slowly reduced. NOTE: the off-shore breeze had shifted almost 180 degrees to an on-shore breeze while we were gabbing about my mortality. I would be attempting to land toward the wet-lands swamp rather than away from the swamp. Welcome to Florida.

Fortunately, an instructor pilot in an identical SNJ joined up and flew a loose formation on my right wing to help to talk me down to a landing by constantly telling me my exact air speed so that I would not lose track, suddenly stall, and fall out of the air at an altitude too low to recover. That way, I was able to keep my head up and on a swivel while descending without running up too much or too little air speed in the process. That's a pretty good trick for a NavCad student pilot who, aside from little more than an hour flying the new Beechcraft T-34 Mentor aircraft that only the Air Force had at that time, and about the same pittance in a much hotter T-28 Trojan aircraft with my CAC brothers.

However, both of those aircraft were equipped with tricycle landing gear while I had only landed SNJ tail-dragging aircraft with a comfortably slow, full-stall landing and not by greasing the aircraft onto the runway Air Force style like I was attempting to do for the very first time.

So I opened my canopy, lowered my seat as far down as it would go, pulled my shoulder and lap harnesses even tighter, said yet another fervent Act of Contrition, asked Holy Joe, my Guardian Angel to get to work on my case muy pronto, and I may have offered up my first-born child in the bargain as well. I'm not sure.

Then I turned very carefully onto my straight-in approach beginning about 15 miles north of the duty runway. Fresh out of options and thoroughly committed to try to land that gut-shot old junker one more time, I muttered "Houkah hei" into my microphone, which is, I believe, shorthand for a Plains Indian adage loosely translated as "this is as good a day to die as any." From our monthly, late-night CAC steak and keg parties, my CAC brother, the Safety Officer, received my message loud and clear. I figured that I had no choice but to go for broke.

Flying at a bit more than 28 knots faster than specifications on my final approach, I knew that I would be darned lucky to touch down in the first third of that very short 6,000-foot north-to-south runway. However, when I tried but could not touch down in the first third at that excessive airspeed, and barely within the second third of that very short runway, I knew that I was in a world of hurt, and that abnormal landing attempt probably would not end well for me.

As my pal Bill Brill's mama often said: "Pain hurts." I just knew that I was not going to get through this ordeal without a heck of a lot of pain.

Actually, I initially touched down somewhere between the second and the final third of the duty runway, but by that time I was too darned close to my new 100-knot stalling speed—the normal stalling speed was about 78 knots—so taking a wave-off to go around and try again was probably not a survivable option at that altitude. So I cut my power completely, banged down on the runway way too hard and too fast, ballooned a couple of times, and passed between two Navy fire trucks that were racing down each side of the runway with their pedals to the metal. At a little more than 100 knots—about 114 miles per hour—I passed between them like they were standing still. Heck, I nearly blew their doors off.

A few seconds later, I bounced over the south end of the runway while still moving at about 110 miles per hour. At that speed, when hurtling through a brackish swamp that was once a densely forested wetland, a junior birdman's future can be measured in seconds. Having no control except for a faint semblance of brakes since I was bouncing along in the air so much, I slammed into a large, sturdy swamp tree that violently snapped me to the right and took off my right wing at the fuselage with a head-banging, neck-popping impact that pretty much boogered every muscle and tendon in my body.

Still standing on the brakes with the joystick anchored back in my lap with both hands, I vaguely remember hitting a second tree at about midpoint on my left wing, which suddenly, violently snapped me in the other direction and tore off that wing as well as the engine cowling and other susceptible parts. That spun me around like a whirling dervish on steroids—maybe a full 360 degrees a couple of times; I really don't know because it happened so fast—which removed my propeller and engine at the lord mounts directly in front of my cockpit cage, and then smashed my entire tail assembly into a whole gaggle of fluttering fragments and metal strips.

Immediately after that, the momentum threw what was left of the cockpit cage with me in it against a huge tree trunk head-on and dropped my SNJ's gaping-open front end down against that tree in at least waist-high, brackish, wet-lands swamp water. That flipped what was left of the torn-up fuselage cage straight forward into an upside-down stack of scrambled parts.

Having been snapped around violently again and again, even though my shoulder and lap harnesses had been tightened and retightened, I was so boogered that I lost all track of time and motion. However, I would guess that the entire destruction of that weary old junker probably took only a few seconds from the point of hitting the first tree and then spinning violently and much too fast in both directions until the sudden, head-snapping stop when I hit the last tree to crush my open canopy and smash against that tree's massive trunk where I mercifully lost all consciousness while hanging upside down with my head and shoulders fully submerged under that black, swamp water.

Thank God for the sturdy crash bar just behind my head, and for that magnificent Navy crash crew in their silver moon suits who got to the scene of the accident almost as soon as I did. All things considered, that was quite a slick trick for them to somehow follow the path that I had cut through that still densely wooded, mud-sucking swamp so quickly, but thank God that they somehow did that trick in what must have been record time.

I do wish that someone had taken a movie to show the world just how great and efficiently those Navy crash crew guys did their very difficult job. But take it from the guy who darned near drowned without even knowing it, I am darned sure that I would not have survived without their fast, efficient, life-saving heroics.

I have vague memories of drifting in and out of consciousness in a world where every part of my body hurt like the dickens while I snorted and puked vile liquids in and out of my nose and mouth as a surge of deep sorrow enveloped me. That was not how I thought heaven would be.

Quickly and efficiently, those crash crew guys in their otherworldly silver suits either released or cut my harness straps to drop me head-first onto something hard and substantial like a stump below the surface of that crappy tasting swamp water. Then, some more Navy guys in firefighting gear appeared out of nowhere and toted me on a stretcher through the swamp to the meat wagon as little patches of gasoline ignited around us on the surface of the vile swamp water. I vaguely remember them as bright flickers on the blackish surface of the shiny swamp water that seemed like hundreds of flickering candles swirling around me. However, the accident report said the fire was a bit more intense than that.

I was so darned glad to be finally on the ground—even mucky, swampy ground—that the encircling thousand "candles" did not bother me at all. To me, they were pretty lights that were somehow really comforting like great big clusters of candles at Midnight Mass on Christmas Eve rather than the solemn serenity of a Requiem Funeral Mass.

With everything finally under Navy control, I drifted off to La La Land again.

Go Navy. I love you guys.

Like Mr. Cowboy, the battered old night clerk at the Royal Hotel in El Dorado, Kansas, often described a hard day of breaking broncos or branding cattle back in his prime: "I felt like I had been rode hard and put away wet." I could not have said it better.

62. YOU SCRATCH MY BACK AND I'LL SCRATCH YOURS.

I awoke in the main Navy hospital at the Pensacola Flight Training Command. As I was recovering from another major concussion as well as many other generally debilitating aches and pains all over my body ("pain hurts!"), the doctors found indisputable evidence of past bruises and abrasions to my noggin in days of yore. Immediately if not sooner, my ticket for further joy-stick time as a Navy/Marine pilot was cancelled.

Heck fire, the evidence of that original damage was apparently there all of the time if anyone had looked during my many physicals, and may still be there today. Then, as they huddled in the hall outside my hospital room, I could hear several of those doctors grumbling about such as: "How in the heck did that guy ever get here in the first place;" as well as harsh incriminations such as "bogus enlistment." I figured that I was in deep kimshii, but was in no condition to get up and run for it.

As I explained ad nauseum that before I enlisted, I reported my medical history as best I could under the circumstances. However, on the repeated advice of my recruiter, Sgt. Kuhn, who filled out my medical record because my writing hand was broken and in a plaster cast from playing junior college football, I did not add anything that was not asked; just like I was told to do. I joined the Marines so that I could go to Korea and get even with the North Korean and Chinese S.O.B's who had killed and wounded several of my good friends back home. It was as simple as that.

After that, everything kind of flowed along too rapidly and beyond my control. Those three unexpected high IQ test scores in one year led to Mensa and sidetracked me to OCS. But that was okay with me after the Cease Fire in Korea ruined Plan A and I did not have a Plan B at that time.

Everyone involved in my last flight got together a couple of days after I was released from the hospital, but I did not see any accident photos so some of those guys figured that those probably were not processed yet. Yeah, right. Additionally, no one told me which son of a bitch flew and boogered that SNJ just before it was passed on to unsuspecting me. I'm absolutely sure that they knew, but no one to my knowledge squealed on him so he had to be someone with a metric pot full of influence. That s**t bird knowingly tore up the control cables' rigging system and the flaps so darned badly, yet he did not report that critical damage as required.

So much for that B.S. NavCad Honor System for reporting major damage to that aircraft. Whose naïve, stupid, cotton-picking idea was that dingbat Honor System, anyway? We are talking life or death, not gentlemen's polo.

However, the Safety Officer, my Confederate Air Corps pal, did verify that the cables, etc. of the whole danged control system were fatally out of rig and there was nothing that I could have done about it after I was in the air. In fact, they figured that I was darned lucky just to get that gut-shot old junker into the air in the first place because I probably should have crashed during takeoff.

I mentioned that they should tell me something that I did not already know, like who the heck flew that aircraft and clobbered it just before my flight, thereby screwing it up so incredibly badly, and then did not file a squawk to get the darned thing overhauled or torn down for spare parts as a shop queen. If I had known that SOB's name, I damned sure would have burned down his barn.

But after all of that was said and done, the thing that really fried my hide the most was why the heck wasn't I diverted from that minimum, inadequate 6,000-foot-long runway at NAS Sauffley Field to the 18,000-foot long runways at Eglin Air Force Base only a few minutes by air to the east of the Pensacola Flight Training Command. I'll bet that I could have flown that beat-up, old hunk of junk directly onto those three-mile long runways—versus our puny little 6,000-foot runway—at a safe airspeed approximating our standard cruising speed. That could have made that 100-knot stalling speed immaterial. If so, I could now be a retired Marine Aviator despite all of my warts, and the U.S. Navy would have had one more gut-shot old junker SNJ to use as a shop queen until the brand new, delightful-to-fly Beechcraft T-34 Mentor aircraft would finally arrive.

Ah well, as they often said in the bowels of the ancient Roman Coliseum: "non illigitimus nehil carborundum." That translates, I believe, to: "Don't let the bastards get you down." Do I hear another "Aaaa-men?" I certainly hope so.

63. AN OFFER I COULD NOT REFUSE

When I was still at the NAS Pensacola hospital, a couple of seasoned Navy officers who showed neither rank nor any identification on their obviously borrowed, ill-fitting, white, hospital coats—but sporting the command presence of top dog authority galore—came to my room, excused the pretty nurse who was giving me a thorough and delightful sponge bath in bed, shut the door, and made me an offer that I could not/better not refuse. Actually, those senior officers did not give me a whole heck of a lot of choice.

Essentially their offer boiled down to me scratching their backs and they reciprocating by scratching mine while simultaneously over-looking my hot-to-trot, naïve young-guy, faux pas while trying to get even with the Chinese and North Korean bad guys. If I agreed to these unidentified officers' offer to join a troubled Navy atom bomber squadron to "observe everything that takes place within sight or hearing," and report back to some other flag officer identified only as "the Boss".

According to these two steely eyed characters, if I played ball with them, I would eventually be discharged as a Marine Staff Sergeant. That would be a huge perk at that time, which I understand became standard for all Marine NavCads who have at least 100 hours of flight time when grounded. But don't quote me on that because I really don't know about that after 63 years of separation. Additionally, I would do no time in the active reserves since I was no longer 1A, and there would be no more flack about my bad/nasty impulsive bogus enlistment just to kill a few bad guys in Korea.

Also, I would get an all-expenses-paid exotic cruise in the beautiful Mediterranean Sea with all of the free coffee that I could drink 24/7, the GI Bill benefits, the VA medical benefits, and other benefits too mentionable to be numerous, or words to that effect.

I didn't know if it was that Mensa thing; or my fairly special relationship with the Admiral during about a year that I was the

Cadet Battalion Commander; or our midnight steak and keg parties every month when Admiral and cadet were both equal colonels in the Confederate Air Corps for a few hours; or because I crammed in time in my already jam-packed schedule to play offensive/defensive end and punter on the Admiral's pride and joy football team; or how well I escorted various VIPs hither and yon when I could have been doing something else like studying or R & R; or when I "shot down" my instructor in a mock dog fight using a trick that I learned from Captain Fisher who was once Pappy Boyington's wingman in the Black Sheep squadron; or when I clobbered that Ivy League boxing instructor/twit in the first round of a three-round boxing demonstration so that he had to be replaced by another instructor who could actually box; or because I'm left handed and had a good tan or what.

Heck, I don't know what it was that lit those senior officers' and gentlemen's fire, but they would not take "No Sir" for their offer. It seemed like they had me by the short hairs. One minute they were all hellfire and brimstone and the next minute they were my future best friends.

When I woke up the next morning, I called the Commanding Officer of the Marine Detachment at Pensacola on the phone to ask for an appointment with him to discuss my shaky options. Unfortunately, the CO was traveling so his secretary/office pinky transferred my call to the Marine Personnel Office where somebody who had a strong vocal command presence but a sympathetic attitude told me that he was sure that I could come back to the Marines right away, but I would need to re-enlist for three more years to do that.

Time was of the essence. I had to make a big decision, and do that right away. We talked for a while, and as an aside the Marine Personnel guy mentioned that since I wanted to get back to college as soon as possible, I would get out in just 10 months if I would take the Navy offer.

Long story short, after quite a bit of give and take, I eventually took those steely eyed Navy guys at their word. Since they had nothing to be signed at that moment, I settled for hand-shakes all around to get rid of them, and took another nap since I was still pretty much used up and hurting. Like Mrs. Brill often said: "Pain hurts."

What the heck, after all was said and done, I did actually owe my life to a couple of hard-charging Navy crash crews and a bunch of Navy corpsmen who just flat did not give up even after I had been under water so darn long. I understand that it was something more than four minutes. Well hell, I have always taken pride in paying off my debts as promptly as possible and, in a way, they wanted something that I could give them right away. So why not

A word to the wise: when negotiating with "officers and gentlemen" like those Navy officer guys, get it in writing. A rookie in such matters: I did not do that. I was just so darned happy to still be breathing and getting private sponge baths. Then, I drifted off to sleep.

64. 1955: VAH-7 SECRET ATOM BOMBER SQUADRON

Little did I initially realize what a bodacious can of worms was dumped on me from somewhere at the apex of the U.S. Navy hierarchy; the intensity of the effort and the time needed to bring myself up to the essential competence needed to pull off this squadron-wide deception and then some; or how much fun I had between occasional startling incidents. Even if I had known the length, width and depth of that covert operation in advance, I would not have missed it for anything; not even when pinned down on the wrong end of an Israeli fire-power demonstration in Jerusalem.

On second thought, I would have gladly done without an attempted murder by a couple of unknown bad guy driving an antique Mercedes limousine on the incredibly narrow lanes deep in the ancient slum on the west side of Istanbul, Turkey. Yeah, come to think of it, I would have gladly missed that very close call.

If you enjoyed the first two books in this Cold War Warrior Trilogy—*1953: Making A Marine Grunt Warrior* and *1954: Making A Marine Pilot Warrior*—and enjoy reading true, action-packed, covert adventures set in the exotic countries surrounding the Mediterranean Sea in 1955, especially about the tinder-box Middle East and the constantly contested Holy Lands, I am confident that you will enjoy *1955: VAH-7 Secret Atom Bomber Squadron*.

65. MILITARY AVIATION QUOTES

a. "When a crash seems inevitable, endeavor to strike the softest, cheapest object in the vicinity as slowly and gently as possible."

Advice given RAF pilots during WW II.

b. "There are old pilots and there are bold pilots, but there are no old, bold pilots."
Signs in all hangars at the Pensacola Training Command in 1954 and 1955.

c. "If a pilot screws up, the pilot dies. If Air Traffic Control screws up, the pilot dies."

That is the difference between pilots and Air Traffic Control.

d. "The only time that you have too much fuel is when you are on fire."

A common aviation axiom.

e. "Flying the airplane is more important than radioing your plight to a person on the ground who is incapable of fully understanding or doing anything about it."

Just plain good sense.

www.ingramcontent.com/pod-product-compliance
Lightning Source LLC
LaVergne TN
LVHW091559060526
838200LV00036B/911